Education
Before School

Education
Before School

INVESTING IN QUALITY CHILD CARE

BY ELLEN GALINSKY
AND DANA S. FRIEDMAN

For the Committee For Economic Development

SCHOLASTIC INC.
NEW YORK   TORONTO   LONDON   AUCKLAND   SYDNEY

Education Before School represents the work of its authors and does not necessarily represent the views of the Trustees of the Committee for Economic Development (CED). CED's views are presented in the policy statement *Why Child Care Matters: Preparing Young Children for a More Productive America*, published separately by the Committee for Economic Development.

Contents

The Committee for Economic Development and the authors of *Education Before School* are most grateful to the following organizations for their support of this publication.

Carnegie Corporation of New York
Champion International Corporation
Corning Incorporated
Dayton Hudson Foundation
E. I. Du Pont de Nemours & Co.
The Ford Foundation
Johnson & Johnson Family of Companies
Kraft General Foods
The John D. & Catherine T. MacArthur Foundation
Primerica Foundation
Smith Richardson Foundation, Inc.
The Stride Rite Corporation

Foreword

C hild care is more than a place where parents can safely leave their children during the workday. As a vital part of the nation's education system, it is a place where our youngest children can begin to develop the fundamental skills that allow them to become lifelong learners and productive workers and citizens. Child care is also an important service for families and employers. Reliable and affordable care allows parents to work more productively.

The Committee for Economic Development's (CED) involvement in the issue of child care stems from a long-standing interest in improving both education and work force policies. Over the past decade, CED has pursued studies on such subjects as school reform, the education of low-income children, and the development of worker skills because it has viewed investment in human resources as an essential element of a strong and competitive economy. Out of this body of work, child care emerged as an important component of the nation's early childhood education system, as well as an issue that can affect the quality of our work force now and in the future.

In order to assess the current state of the nation's child care system, CED commissioned Ellen Galinsky and Dana Friedman, Copresidents of the Families and Work Institute, to prepare a research report that could serve as background for further CED policy work on child care. This book, *Education Before School: Investing in Quality Child Care*, is the result of their efforts. CED subsequently appointed a subcommittee of trustees, which I had the honor of chairing, charged with formulating policy recommendations for improving the nation's child care system. The result of our subcommittee's work is the CED policy statement: *Why Child Care Matters: Preparing Young Children for a More Productive America*. We are pleased to be releasing both the research report and the policy statement simultaneously.

The research report *Education Before School* views child care as an important opportunity to foster the healthy development and education of all of our children from the very earliest stages of life — particularly in an era of shifting demographics and a rapidly changing economy. It underscores the strong link between the quality of children's early care and education and the possibility of school reform. Unless more attention is paid to the experiences children have before they arrive at school, it is doubtful that our nation's efforts to restructure its education system will succeed. *Education Before School* describes the stake that every sector of society holds in helping to strengthen our nation's child care system.

In *Education Before School*, Ms. Galinsky and Dr. Friedman provide an enormous amount of data never before presented in a single volume. They describe the many forms of child care, the quality and availability of care, the functioning of the child care market, and the programs government uses to support the market. There is a special emphasis in the report on what business can do to address the child care needs of employees and the needs of the larger community. Many companies have found that it is a worthwhile investment to provide child care for their employees or to help support employee child care needs in other ways. Some businesses have also begun to realize that child care that puts children on the road to successful learning and helps them become ready for formal schooling can contribute to a pool of qualified workers tomorrow. The report thus contains numerous case studies of successful corporate initiatives to improve child care.

The CED policy statement, *Why Child Care Matters,* follows up on the background information presented in Ms. Galinsky and Dr. Friedman's research and puts forth recommendations for improving child care policies that carry the full weight of the business leaders who worked on this report. We hope that policy makers, business executives, educators, and the public will be able to use *Why Child Care Matters* and *Education Before School* as companion pieces.

We are most grateful to Ms. Galinsky and Dr. Friedman for the insight, expertise, and knowledge they brought to the research report, as well as for their participation in the preparation of the policy statement, where they offered invaluble advice.

Robert E. Campbell
Vice Chairman
Johnson & Johnson

Acknowledgments

The authors are most grateful for the substantive guidance and editorial assistance offered by the staff of the Committee for Economic Development, who reviewed countless drafts of this book. We especially thank Sol Hurwitz, Van Doorn Ooms, Sandra Kessler Hamburg, Julie Won, and Michael Greenstone.

We gratefully acknowledge the invaluable research and editorial assistance of Wendy Gray, Carol Shookhoff, Catherine Morrison, May Beth Ostendorf Harvey, Laurie Kane, Leslie Gates, Veronica Plowden, Laura Hankin, and Robin Hardman.

The following child care and business experts contributed their knowledge and insights to this report:

Gina Adams, Children's Defense Fund, Washington, DC; Allen Bergerson, Retired, Eastman Kodak Company, Rochester, NY; James T. Bond, Families and Work Institute, New York, NY; Richard Clifford, Frank Porter Graham Child Development Center, University of North Carolina,

Chapel Hill, NC; Jerlean Daniel, University of Pittsburgh, Pittsburgh, PA; Sarah Gomez, IBM, Purchase, NY; Wendy Gray, Independent Consultant, Wanamassa, NJ; Sharon Lynn Kagan, Yale University, New Haven, CT; Sheila Kamerman, Columbia University School of Social Work, New York, NY; John Kyle, National League of Cities, Washington, DC; Joan Lombardi, Early Childhood Policy Analyst, Alexandria, VA; Lynn Manfredi-Pettit, National Association for Family Day Care, Atlanta, GA; Anne Mitchell, Early Childhood Policy Researcher, Climax, NY; Gwen Morgan, Wheelock College and Work/Family Directions, Boston, MA; Deborah Phillips, University of Virginia, Charlottesville, VA; Barbara Reisman, Child Care Action Campaign, New York, NY; Fran Rodgers, Work/Family Directions, Boston, MA; Deborah Stahl, AT&T, Morristown, NJ; Eleanor Szanton, Zero to Three, National Center for Clinical Infant Program, Alexandria, VA; Marjorie Warlick, Child Care Resources, Inc., Charlotte, NC; Barbara Willer, National Association for the Education of Young Children, Washington, DC; Faith Wohl, Du Pont Company, Wilmington, DE; Edward F. Zigler, Yale University, New Haven, CT.

We are particularly grateful to Sandra Hofferth of The Urban Institute; Kathy Modigliani of Wheelock College; Barbara Willer of the National Association for the Education of Young Children; Joan Lombardi, an early childhood policy analyst; Mary Culkin, Suzanne W. Helburn, and John R. Morris of the University of Colorado at Denver; and Tom Copeland of Resources for Child Caring for their contributions toward estimating the cost of care.

We also want to thank Sasha Frère-Jones, Robin O'Hara, and Barbara Norcia for their word processing and graphic design assistance.

Introduction

If one word could characterize the advent of the twenty-first century, that word would be *change*. There will be changes in the workplace and in family life that will make the twenty-first-century landscape vastly different from today's.

In anticipation of these changes, society is focusing on young children. No longer simply sentimentalized, children have become the subject of fierce congressional debates, presidential and even world summit conferences, business and news magazine cover stories, and television news shows. One in ten children is born chemically addicted, one in five is condemned to the devastating cycle of poverty, one in four fails to graduate from high school, and one in four, although a graduate, is still functionally illiterate. The population of children is smaller than in the past (the baby bust generation), and business, community, and government leaders are beginning to recognize that we simply cannot afford these losses.

The failure to invest in children and their early education and development is a failure to invest in our own productive future, a failure that will cost us dearly. One of the more important events in the history of business involvement in early education was the 1987 publication of *Children in Need: Investment Strategies for the Educationally Disadvantaged* by the Committee for Economic Development. As that report so eloquently stated:

> Quality education is not an expense; it is an investment in the future of our nation . . . .
> Failure to educate is the true expense — for both society and individuals.[1]

Business leaders recognize that the economy of the twenty-first century will call for new skills. They see that much of our educational system — with its emphasis on sitting still, memorizing the correct answer, and reciting it back — provides skills needed for an assembly-line economy, but not for a world in which technology is rapidly developing and communication skills and literacy are critical. In the future, employees will need to be lifelong learners who can solve problems not thought of a few years before. Employees will also need to be able to collaborate with an increasingly diverse work force. As stated in the National Education Goals formulated by President Bush and the National Governors' Association in 1990:

> Our people must be as knowledgeable, as well trained, as competent, and as inventive as those in any other nation. All of our people, not just a few, must be able to think for a living, adapt to changing environments, and understand the world around them. They must continually learn and develop new skills throughout their lives.[2]

If we are to have this kind of competitive world-class work force in the future, we need to work now to ensure that our nation's children grow up to be productive workers and responsible citizens. For this reason, the first goal of the National Education Goals states, "By the year 2000, all children in America will start school ready to learn." The leaders of our country recognized that this country must find better ways to invest in the earliest years of children's lives, must offer access to developmentally appropriate preschool programs, must support parents as children's first teachers, and better coordinate early education with social services and health services for children and their families.

LINKING EDUCATION AND CARE

In a period of social flux, reality sometimes moves faster than our assumptions about it. Inevitably, once-valid assumptions become obsolete. In the public debate about young children, and meeting the Readiness Goal, there is one assumption that is no longer true, if it ever was: that schools provide education and child care provides care. By "education," we refer to the learning that occurs as children interact and engage in experiences and activities. The definition of "care" goes beyond custodial giving and includes nurturing.

While it is widely believed that children receive education in schools, and child care is merely custodial, a 1989 study of early childhood programs and the public schools conducted by Bank Street College and Wellesley College found this to be far from the truth.[3] In comparing public school and community-based child care programs for four-year-olds, they found that the sponsorship of a program was not the determining factor of whether or not the program promoted children's learning or rated highly on the Early Childhood Environment Rating Scale (ECERS), a measure of the quality of the environment of the educational setting.

Likewise, the National Research Council of the National Academy of Sciences, in its meticulous review of the research, also concluded:

> High-quality and low-quality care can be found among all types of services, whether they are provided in the child's home or outside it, in schools, child care centers, or family child care homes, in programs operated for profit or those operated not for profit.[4]

It is the quality of the program that matters, not the building in which the program is housed, nor the auspices under which it is run.

Children are always learning—whether in the care of teachers at school or in the care of parents, relatives, or nonrelatives at home, family child care homes, or child care centers. One cannot turn off and on a child's mind so that only in certain settings children are learning. If there is one point we hope to emphasize in this book, it is that if we as a nation are to meet the Readiness Goal, we must realize that child care forms a major portion of the early education system in this country.

Implications of Splitting Education and Care

The implications of splitting education and care are not merely semantic. Seeing the two as separate clouds policy decisions. In the enthusiasm to address the needs of young children, programs are created and directions charted that may have negative consequences in the future. Among these are:

An emphasis on preschool children that ignores the needs of infants and toddlers. Due to limited funding, public educational efforts have been targeted to four-year-olds. The National Education Goals state: "Our policy must be to provide at least one year of preschool for all disadvantaged children."[5] In fact, it is important to provide good-quality opportunities throughout the preschool years. It is very difficult to intervene successfully at age four when a child has spent three years in a poor-quality setting.[6] If we as a nation do not find ways to provide developmentally appropriate experiences for the numerous infants and toddlers who are in child care, we will certainly pay the price later on.

An emphasis on school programs that ignores available community resources. As states begin to invest in early childhood programs, some are putting all their resources into school-based ones, sometimes ignoring excellent programs in community-based settings. Often, a considerable amount of public dollars is invested in such programs. While there are some very creative models for using schools as the hub of the early childhood care system, efforts to improve quality must include community-based programs as well.

An emphasis on part-day school programs that ignores the needs of families for full-day programs. Because school-based programs are typically part-day, they increase the complexity of the child care arrangements employed parents must make for their children. The subsequent lack of continuity for children could jeopardize their development. Some states think they have solved this problem with the creation of wrap-around programs, i.e., a school-based educational program with a child care component covering additional hours when parents are at work. This program inappropriately assumes that a child's day can be divided into learning and nonlearning times. Rather, children are always learning. It further creates a two-tiered system, with teachers in child care settings earning lower wages than teachers of the same-age children in school settings. Lower wages often lead to high turnover and diminishing quality. Michigan, Colorado, and Oregon, among other states, have shown that it is possible to create part-day and full-day options within both schools and community-based child care programs.

An emphasis on extending education downward in inappropriate ways. In many states, interest in early education has triggered an increased emphasis on a "drill-and-practice" curriculum, ignoring the fact that young children learn abstract concepts and skills through meaningful concrete experiences. Fortunately, the National Education Goals recognize the shortcomings of the drill-and-practice approach and call for "developmentally appropriate programs."

An emphasis on school-based learning that ignores parental involvement. Education is often viewed narrowly. While many believe that parents should stay informed, help their children with home-

6

work, and come to PTA meetings, the teacher should be left alone to teach. Yet, the research on early childhood programs has shown that active parent involvement is critical to program success and positive child outcomes. As the National Education Goals recognize, the parent is the "child's first teacher." Programs must build on that base, not try to supplant it, especially in the earliest years.

An emphasis on serving those most in need that labels or stigmatizes children or families or creates de facto segregation. It is understandable that limited resources be targeted to those most in need, but the unintended consequence is often to create a separate tier of services for low-income and minority children. The children become known as the "at-risk" group, a label that is very hard to shake. The emphasis must be on giving parents a diversity of good and affordable child care choices that are appropriately educational. The approach must be preventative and holistic.

An emphasis on learning that ignores families' needs for comprehensive services. One out of every ten children in America is born chemically addicted. One in five comes from a low-income home. While early education programs cannot inoculate against these problems, a comprehensive approach that addresses the broad needs of children and their families, linking families to the social services they need, is more effective than a narrow one.

An emphasis on preparing children for schools that ignores the need for schools to prepare for

the children. Good-quality preschool care and education programs cannot, by themselves, prevent later school failure. Unless significant efforts are made to have good-quality, developmentally appropriate elementary and secondary schools — where activities are geared to the age and skills of the child — the gains of early childhood education and care will disappear. Experimentation is needed, including curriculum reform, the creation of early childhood units within schools, and encouragement of coordination between the public schools and the early childhood field.[7]

Two out of every five American children under the age of five, with both employed and nonemployed mothers, are in nonrelative child care settings.[8] **Thus, if educational reform is to succeed, and this country is to meet the Readiness Goal, business and government leaders need to recognize that quality child care is the foundation of the education system, and will contribute to the later school success of children.**

When the educational value of child care is taken into account, child care becomes an important and multifaceted issue, affecting society, business, parents, and children, both now and in the future. Now, the quality and availability of child care affects our labor force. The reliability of child care arrangements can affect the productivity of employed parents, with unreliable care leading to higher absenteeism, tardiness, and stress on the job. In the future, the 51 percent of children under the age of five with employed mothers currently in nonrelative care will be our labor pool, and the quality of the care and education they receive now will affect their physical, social, emotional, and cognitive development.

In an age of chemical addiction, poverty, families under stress, and schools in crisis, this means that child care has the potential to play a major role in building up our nation's human capital in the long run.

This book recognizes child care as an important human resource, public policy, and educational issue. It revolves around the gap between child care as custodial care and child care as early education, and it emphasizes what we call high-quality child care, which we define as care and "developmentally appropriate" education: that is, education that takes full account of what we know about the way children learn.

High-quality care, however, is expensive, and raising quality means raising price, most likely beyond the range of the average-income parent. This book explores the trade-offs between high quality and cost. It asks policy makers and business leaders to consider what can be done for parents who cannot afford high-quality care on their own, as well as for those parents who can afford it but are not willing to pay for it because they are not aware of the difference it can make in their children's lives later on.

Chapter 1, "An Introduction to Child Care, Quality, and the Stakes," explains why child care issues are so important and describes some of the demographic trends that will increase the demand for child care. It also defines child care and what we mean by "high-quality" child care.

Chapter 2, "Child Care Problems," describes the state of our current child care "system" and its biggest problems. These range from the difficulty parents face in finding child care, to poor information on child care options and "barely adequate programs."

Chapter 3, "The Benefits of Typical and High-Quality

Child Care," describes the benefits that child care, particularly high-quality care, can bring to business, parents, children, and society.

Chapter 4, "The Cost of Typical and High-Quality Child Care," estimates the full cost of providing higher quality and explores the hard choices that accompany higher cost.

Chapter 5, "The Response from Government and Business," looks at private and public sector responses to child care problems, as well as the public's ambivalence toward child care.

Chapter 6, "Conclusion," lays out the authors' suggested policy guidelines for child care.

Unfortunately, no book can cover everything. By focusing on high quality and questions linked to quality, we were not able to discuss many other important child care issues in these pages. For instance, this book does not cover the role child care can play in helping families escape welfare dependency, a topic others have examined.[9]

Finally, we examine federal and state government involvement in child care. However, since this book was commissioned by a business group, the Committee for Economic Development, a slightly greater emphasis is placed on the positive role that business can play in helping to improve the delivery of child care. As a result, Chapter 5 includes numerous case studies of creative and successful corporate initiatives, as well as of corporate partnerships with community or government. This in no way implies that business has the societal responsibility for solving our nation's child care dilemma. In our view, the role of business is to build on the solid infrastructure that local, state, and national governments create.

Our hope is that both business and government will use this book as a reference for their own initiatives to improve child care for their employees or constituencies. We also hope the book might provide an incentive for business and government to devise creative solutions to some of the many problems we still need to resolve.

REFERENCES

1. Committee for Economic Development, *Children in Need: Investment Strategies for the Educationally Disadvantaged* (New York: CED, 1987).

2. National Governors' Association, "National Education Goals" (Washington, DC: National Governors' Association, February 25, 1990).

3. A. Mitchell, M. Seligson, and F. Marx, *Early Childhood Programs and the Public Schools: Between Promise and Practice* (Boston: Auburn House, 1989).

4. C. D. Hayes, J. L. Palmer, and M. L. Zaslow, eds., *Who Cares for America's Children? Child Care Policy for the 1990s* (Washington, DC: National Academy Press, 1990, p. xii).

5. National Governors' Association.

6. C. Howes, M. Shinn, L. M. Sakai, D. Phillips, E. Galinsky, and M. Whitebook, *Race, Social Class, and Maternal Working Conditions as Influences on Children's Development in Child Care* (Los Angeles: UCLA, in preparation).

7. "Caring Communities: Supporting Young Children and Families," *The Report of the National Task Force on School Readiness* (Alexandria, VA: National Association of State Boards of Education, December 1991).

8. S. L. Hofferth, A. Brayfield, S. Deitch, and P. Holcomb, *The National Child Care Survey* (Washington, DC: The Urban Institute, 1991).

9. S. Smith, S. Blank, and J. T. Bond, *One Program, Two Generations* (New York: Foundation for Child Development and National Center for Children and Poverty, 1990).

CHAPTER I

An Introduction to Child Care, Quality, and the Stakes

A clear definition of what child care is and is not can be confusing to federal policy makers, state regulators, researchers, educators, employers, parents, and the public. Many do not understand what child care providers do, how child care and preschool or school are related, and how programs like Head Start fit in. Programs can be characterized by location, type of provider, hours of operation, funding source, and auspices. What is a full-day program that calls itself a preschool? Is it child care or not? What is full-day Head Start or a family child care arrangement used by a nonemployed mother?

At the same time our confusion grows, child care is becoming increasingly important, and our stake in the kind of nonparental care children receive is rising. What happens to children in their earliest years, from birth or even the prenatal stage to age five, is important to their development. Currently, two out of every five children under the age of five, of both employed and nonemployed mothers, are in the care of a nonrelative,[1] and a three-year-old in full-time child care from 8:00 A.M. to 6:00 P.M. may be spending more than half of his or her waking hours during the week in the care of adults other than his or her parents.[2] The stakes will continue to rise as the size and composition of our work force change — particularly as the number of employed mothers grows.

Business has begun to realize the stakes involved in both the short and long term. In the short term, child care affects the productivity of working parents. It is no longer possible for workers to leave their personal problems at home, as most company cultures still dictate, because there is rarely someone at home to solve them. More than one third of the labor force now is composed of working parents. Their needs must be addressed to a greater extent than in the past if companies are to recruit and retain a productive work force in an increasingly competitive marketplace. In the longer term, the quality of care children receive could have an effect on our future labor pool and our citizens. We know that the quality of care that children receive — whether from parents or nonparents — can affect their social, cognitive, and physical development. We also know that our labor force is shrinking and that children who grow up unable to participate in a technologically complex world become losses that we can no longer afford.

THE IMPETUS: CHANGING DEMOGRAPHICS

Changing demographics have triggered a growing interest in early education and care, particularly within the corporate community. The labor force will grow by 17 percent in the years between 1985 and 2000, compared with the 40 percent growth that occurred between 1970 and 1985.[3] Part of this decline is due to lower birth rates following the increase in fertility rates between 1945 and 1960, which created an excess supply of workers who began to enter the labor force in the 1960s. Today, the youngest "baby boomers" are about thirty years old and represent the tail end of that excess supply.

Population growth, which was 1.9 percent per year in the 1950s, is expected to fall to 0.7 percent per year by the year 2000.[4] In addition, not only will there be fewer younger people, but many of them will have grown up in poverty, dropped out of school, or will be functionally illiterate. They may be unprepared to enter the work force or perform up to the standards required for available jobs.

Among the most profound changes in the labor force is the increase in the percentage of employed mothers with very young children. Between 1950 and 1985, the percentage of mothers with children under the age of six, who were employed, jumped from 12 percent to 54 percent. In 1975, 34 percent of mothers with children under age three were employed.[5] By 1988, the figure had risen to 52 percent, and the 1990 figure is 54 percent.[6] By the year 2000, gender differences in employment will shrink to the point where women will represent 47 percent of all workers.[7]

An important consequence of these trends is that more families now have both parents at work for most of the day. Sixty-six percent of married working men have employed wives. In 61 percent of married-couple families with children under age thirteen, both spouses are in the labor force. Among female-headed households with children under age fifteen, nearly 53 percent of the women have jobs outside the home, as do 73 percent of those with children aged five to twelve.[8] The net result is that most parents of children under eighteen work, and they constitute 38 percent of the labor force.[9]

A Word About Choices

Before going on, it should be made clear that the authors in no way endorse or encourage a particular family life-style, early childhood program choice, or employment pattern. Not all parents need or want child care beyond the family. Many families have chosen to forgo the additional income so that a parent can stay home with the children. In others, parents work different shifts in order that one parent is always with the child. In 28 percent of families with employed mothers and the youngest child under five, parents provide most of the child's care (11 percent by their mothers and 17 percent by their fathers). However, a growing number of couples and employed single parents do need other child care arrangements. In addition, an increasing number of families with at-home mothers send their children to a nursery school, preschool program, or child care center to expose them to other children and a stimulating environment (33 percent).[10]

The authors strongly believe that families must be respected, whatever their choices. There should be respect for families in which the mothers are at home, and those in which the mothers are at work. Neither should be made to feel disapproval, guilt, or pressure to take the other path.

Recruitment

During this decade, companies will have to compete for a shrinking number of workers, many of whom will be women, foreign-born, minority, elderly, or physically challenged. The needs of these new entrants will play a role in their decisions on whether or not they enter the labor force and for whom they work. One aspect of staying competitive could mean restructuring policies and reward systems designed for a traditional, homogeneous work force in order to meet the needs of a new, diverse work force.

In a 1990 nationwide survey conducted by the Families and Work Institute, 55 percent of the largest 188 Fortune 1000 companies in 30 industry areas said that they expected to face labor shortages.[11] In a 1989–1990 survey of employers of all sizes in four states, the Families and Work Institute found that overall, 40 percent of these firms are already finding job vacancies difficult to fill, and 50 percent are finding job vacancies in highly skilled positions difficult to fill, although this trend may have been somewhat reversed by the 1991–1992 recession.[12]

Women will provide almost two thirds of the net increase in the work force between now and the twenty-first century.[13] In addition, the majority of women in the currently available labor pool are in their childbearing years, and most will have children during their work careers. However, child care problems also hamper the recruitment of women to senior-level positions. Only an estimated 35 percent of women in senior positions have children, as opposed to the vast majority of men in similar positions.[14–16] If women are not hired or promoted into top management positions, companies will not be recruiting from a complete pool of talent for the highest levels of management. Felice Schwartz, president of Catalyst, an organization committed to women in management, said at a 1988 Conference Board conference, Women in the Corporation:

> Companies that are determined to recruit the
> same number of men as they are used to

recruiting for leadership positions will have to dig much deeper into the male pool. . . . Even those employers who are reluctant to have women in their upper management ranks will recognize that it is preferable to have high performing women than moderately performing men.[17]

Minority groups are another dimension of the recruiting issue. They will double their share of the labor pool between now and the turn of the century. Although the labor shortage would normally provide openings for minority groups, it has been noted that many minorities are concentrated in economically declining cities with fewer job opportunities.[18] In addition, a disproportionate number of minority women are single mothers. More research will have to be done on the needs, expectations, and family cultures of new immigrant populations, minority workers, and low-income families.

WHAT IS CHILD CARE?

We use Figure 1.1 to show the entire child care landscape, which classifies care and education by location, provider, hours of operation, funding source, and auspice.

Researchers have in the past debated whether public and private schools can be classified as "child care arrangements," as stated in Figure 1.1. Some researchers have regarded the schools as an "informal" source of child care and place them in the same category as caregiving,[34-36] while others have disregarded various school arrangements, as serving any kind of child care function—including nursery

Figure 1.1
EARLY CHILDHOOD PROGRAM DISTINCTIONS

LOCATION	
In-Home	The child learns and is cared for in his or her own home. Three percent of the children who are under five with employed mothers are in nonrelative in-home care.[19]
Family Child Care	Child care is provided for up to 5 or 6 children in the home of the provider. In group family child care, up to 10 or 12 children are cared for in the home of the provider with the assistance of another adult. Twenty percent of the children under five with employed mothers are in family child care, with nonrelatives.[20]
Center	The child learns and is cared for in a child care center. Centers generally refer to full-day programs. Putting centers, nursery schools, and preschools together, 28 percent of children under five with employed mothers use some type of center-based care, including nursery schools and preschools.[21]
Nursery School	Nursery schools typically offer part-day programs. Some nursery schools have extended hours, providing full working day education and care.
School	Fifty-one percent of three- and four-year-olds are in public and private prekindergarten and kindergarten programs. Ninety percent of five-year-olds attend school, 70 percent in public schools, generally for part-day programs.[22,23] Schools also provide before- and after-school programs.
Church/ Synagogue	The program takes place at the site of a religious organization, sometimes sponsored by the denomination and sometimes simply housed there. While up to 60 percent of center-based child care is located in religious organizations, only 15 percent are sponsored by churches or synagogues.[24,25]
Workplace	The program is housed at or near the parents' workplace. This is called on-site or near-site care. In 1990, 13 percent of the nation's largest employers sponsored on- or near-site child care centers. They may be owned and operated by the company or by an outside contractor.[26]

HOURS OF OPERATION	
24-Hour	The program is open round the clock. Sometimes used by hospitals and police departments whose employees work all night and day. Such programs are quite rare.
Full Working Day	The program's hours match the parents' scheduled work hours. Usually the program is open from 7:30 A.M. to 6:00 P.M., but can vary, depending on employee need. Overall, 94 percent of regulated family child care homes and 69 percent of centers provide full working day coverage.[27]
Full School Day	The program's hours are from 9:00 A.M. to 3:00 P.M. or otherwise match the hours that local public schools are open.
Part School Day	Such programs are open two to three hours, in the mornings or afternoons.

Source: Families and Work Institute, 1993.

Figure 1.1—Continued

PROVIDERS	
The terms *teachers* and *child care providers* are sometimes used interchangeably.	
Relative	Eighteen percent of children under five who are the youngest among their siblings, and whose mothers work, are cared for by relatives, and 28 percent by the parents themselves.[28]
Nonrelative	Neighbors, friends, and professionals unrelated to the child are used by just over half of the employed mothers with children under five.
FUNDING SOURCE	
Parents	Parents pay 76 percent of center-based child care.[29]
Local, State, and Federal Governments	Of the estimated $18 billion child care industry (including fees, referrals, licensing, etc.) the federal government contributed approximately $7.7 billion, including the additional $1.1 billion from new federal child care legislation that reached the states.[30,31] It is hard to determine state and local spending because consistent records are not kept.
Employers	Employers may subsidize employees' child care expenses directly or use a tax mechanism to help parents offset costs. Corporate contributions to local child care programs may reduce fees charged to parents.
United Way	In 1990, 7.1 percent of total giving to United Way was allocated to child care.[32]
AUSPICES	
Nonprofit	Sixty-five percent of child care centers are nonprofit, 35 percent are for-profit.[33]

Note: For comparability with previous studies, all figures cited from the National Child Care Survey 1990 refer to the youngest child.

Source: Families and Work Institute, 1993.

schools and kindergartens—and do not consider them in their analyses.[37, 38] Parent definitions of child care also vary. In one study, employed parents were asked a seemingly simple question: "Do you use child care?" Some parents said yes and listed such diverse arrangements as nursery school, kindergarten, Head Start, or grade schools.[39]

At the heart of this confusion is the historical dichotomy between child care and early childhood education. Child care was originally developed to care for the children of low-income families whose mothers had to work, whereas early childhood education was developed as preschool preparation for well-to-do children. These perceived differences are illustrated in Figure 1.2.

Although the debate about the distinctions between education and care still continues in policy-making circles and in public forums, influencing the direction of programs as discussed in the Introduction, it has been more or less settled among researchers with the publication of the 1990 National Child Care Survey.[40] Assuming that the distinctions among types of programs had been blurred by practice, Sandra Hofferth and her colleagues included preschools, nursery schools, Head Start programs, and centers in one classification called "centers" (as we reflect in Figure 1.1). With the publication of this book, *Education Before School*, we hope to extend this understanding more widely—that high-quality child care is both educational and nurturing.

WHAT IS HIGH-QUALITY CHILD CARE?

What then are the determining factors of quality?

High-quality child care recognizes that children are always learning and strives to stimulate this learning process

Figure 1.2

PERCEPTIONS OF THE EARLY CHILDHOOD LANDSCAPE

EARLY CHILDHOOD EDUCATION	CHILD CARE
Characteristic Descriptions	
Is an education service	Is a social welfare program
Essentially for the middle class and affluent	Established to serve lower-class and poor children
A service for intact families	A service for pathological families
Operates in a school or center	Occurs in an institution
Is mainly a service for children	Is mainly a service for parents
Is a supplement to home care	Is substitute care — or worse, custodial care
Is privately funded	Is publicly funded
Operates only a few hours a day	Enrolls children for long hours every day
Human Needs Served	
Provides education and training — enriches the lives of children	Provides care and protection — keeps children from harming others and themselves (starting fires, having accidents)
Encourages value choice and decision making	Imposes values and instills behavior patterns
Encourages freedom and accepts diversity	Imposes conformity
Serves as a family support	Weakens the family
Democratizes children	"Sovietizes" children

Source: B. M. Caldwell, "A Comprehensive Model for Integrating Child Care and Early Childhood Education," *Teachers' College Record*, Vol. 90, No. 3 (1989), pp. 404–414.

through activities that foster social, emotional, and intellectual development. In this book, a high-quality child care program is one that makes the healthy development and education of children its first objective.

Although it may seem that "quality" is hard to define, measure, and provide, research has identified its compo-

22

nents, which remain the same whether the name on the door is Child Care, School, or Preschool. The National Association for the Education of Young Children (NAEYC) has developed standard measures of quality for group care programs for young children based on a thorough review of the research.[41] These standards have been reconfirmed by the National Academy of Sciences' recent review.[42] NAEYC has also developed an accreditation system for center-based care. By 1992, nearly 2,150 programs had become accredited, and 6,000 more were in the process; this means that within the first seven years of available accreditation, 10 percent of America's early childhood programs had participated in this accreditation system. The family child care field is in the process of developing its own accreditation system through the National Association for Family Day Care (NAFDC). At the present time several models exist, but child care leaders are working to consolidate these into one standard.

The single factor that most affects a child's development is the relationship between the child and the teacher-caregiver. Certain aspects of program design, namely, the number of children allowed in a group, the number of children per teacher, and teacher-caregiver education and training, all make a positive relationship more likely. In addition, any good child care program must attend to basic issues of health and safety, and must emphasize a partnership between parents and teachers.

The Relationship Between Child and Caregiver

THE PERSONAL RELATIONSHIP

The most important ingredient of quality care is the relationship between the child and the caregiver—whether a teacher in a center, a family child care provider, or an in-home caregiver.

Studies have found that children form strong attachments to their caregivers, although their attachments to their parents are preeminent.[43] Children who have a secure attachment to both their parents and their caregivers behave more competently than those with one or more insecure attachments to these key figures.[44] Poor relations between caregiver and child can result in a child's feeling of being one among many rather than being treated as an individual, which is one of the foundations of emotional and social well-being.

THE TEACHING RELATIONSHIP

Regardless of the setting, caregivers are teaching children every moment, both formally and informally, and the method of this teaching makes a difference in children's development. Phillips, McCartney, and Scarr found that when children were talked to, asked questions, and encouraged to express themselves, their social development was enhanced, they were more likely to be considerate, and they were also rated as more intelligent and task-oriented. The teaching environment was, in fact, more predictive of the children's achievement than was their social class.[45] In a reanalysis of these data, it was found that children in a verbally stimulating environment were more likely to achieve higher scores on tests of cognitive abilities and language development.[46]

David Weikart, of the High/Scope Foundation and one of the principal investigators of the long-term impact of early childhood programs, prescribes "an explicit, validated child-development curriculum approach," which he defines as "a supportive environment in which children choose their own learning activities and take responsibility for completing them."[47]

NAEYC has coined the term *developmentally appropriate* to describe teaching based on a knowledge of how children learn, specifically through opportunities for direct experience, and for synthesizing this experience through activities such as play, block building, writing, drawing, and painting. One way that NAEYC has disseminated developmentally appropriate teaching is by making it a mainstay of its accreditation process. The National Child Care Staffing Study compared NAEYC accredited centers to others and found that they were superior on all dimensions of quality. In particular, they provided better activities and had teachers who were more sensitive and less severe.[48]

When programs are not developmentally appropriate, children are likely to feel either bored or pressured. In one longitudinal study, it was found that four-year-olds who attended programs in which they spent time aimlessly wandering around were more likely to have developmental problems at eight years of age, including less acceptance by peers, less social competence, and poorer conflict resolution skills.[49] Conversely, when preschool children are overly pressured, elementary school burnout may result.[50]

THE DISCIPLINARY RELATIONSHIP

The disciplinary techniques that parents or other caregivers use affect children's development. Children are more likely to develop self-control and to become more compliant, cooperative, and considerate of the feelings of others if reasoning is used, if providers explain how a child's behavior affects others, and if problem-solving skills are taught. Vandell and

Powers found that when this happens, children have many more positive interactions with staff than they do in lower-quality programs.[51]

There is evidence from child development research that children with insecure attachments to their parents can become more aggressive than other children later on. Although these studies did not focus on children in child care, this finding led some researchers to speculate that perhaps nonparental care led to greater aggression. They based this speculation on two unrelated sets of studies — one showing that children in nonparental care may have a greater likelihood of becoming insecurely attached, and the other showing that children with child care experiences may be more likely to be aggressive.[52–54] Increasingly, researchers are doubting that child care is a direct cause, since it is possible to reduce or eliminate this effect through appropriate handling of aggressive acts. For example, one longitudinal study of children in an intervention program at the University of North Carolina found that children who attended programs from infancy on were more aggressive toward other children upon entering public kindergarten. The North Carolina researchers then developed a curriculum specifically to teach social skills, to replace the current "haphazard process of randomly praising appropriate and punishing inappropriate behavior."[55] With this systematic approach, they were able to reduce the number of aggressive acts by 90 percent. Subsequent assessments of the children who experienced this curriculum found them no more aggressive than the children with no child care experience. Finkelstein concluded that when caregivers are trained in behavior management techniques, the frequency of children's aggressive acts is reduced.[56]

THE STABILITY OF THE RELATIONSHIP

With the high staff turnover that exists in many centers, it is no wonder that a four-year-old recently said to a teacher, "I don't have to listen to you. I was here before you came and I'll still be here when you leave." Some parents report that their children resist going to child care because they simply do not know who will care for them that day. Children have a much easier time separating from their mothers and fathers when they know their caregivers and are in small groups.[57] In studies of family child care, children who changed arrangements frequently were less competent in their interactions with materials and with other children.[58] The National Child Care Staffing Study found that children in programs with high staff turnover achieved less in social and language development.[59]

Program Resources

The second aspect of quality early childhood arrangements relates to resources: group size, staff-child ratio, training opportunities for staff, and health and safety considerations. These resources do not by themselves guarantee high quality, but make it statistically more likely that a positive relationship between the child and the teacher-caregiver will occur.

GROUP SIZE AND STAFF-CHILD RATIO

In the late 1970s, the federal government funded the National Day Care Study to investigate the degree to which regulated features of child care arrangements had an effect on children's development. One of its most important findings was that the group size made a significant difference. In smaller groups the adults spent more time interacting

dren and less time simply watching them. The
e more verbal, more involved in activities, and
___ aggressive. Finally, the children in the smaller groups
made the greatest gains in standardized tests of learning
and vocabulary.[60]

In contrast, the National Child Care Staffing Study
(NCCSS) found small group size to be less important for
enhancing children's development than high staff-child ratios, developmentally appropriate activities, and teachers
who were more sensitive and less severe or detached.[61]
Whichever comes first, both group size and staff-child ratios,
and their combination, are important in creating a high-
quality environment. For instance, when there is a staff-
child ratio of 1:4 in a group of 12 children and 3 teachers
with toddlers (12–24 months), quality is maintained. However, with the same 1:4 ratio in a group of 24 children and
6 teachers, quality diminishes.

The National Day Care Study also found that the number
of adults per child mattered a great deal for infants. Poorer
ratios were correlated with increased emotional distress
and less pro-social behavior.[62] A study of family child care
homes also showed that children in smaller groups were
more verbal, played more, and showed less distress.[63]

NAEYC's accreditation standards, which have gained the
support of both the early childhood field and the research
review conducted by the National Academy of Sciences, use
the staff-child criteria shown in Figure 1.3.

TRAINING AND EDUCATION OF THE CAREGIVER
The National Day Care Study concluded that one of the most
important ingredients of quality was ongoing, relevant training for teacher-caregivers.[64] In programs in which the teachers
had early childhood training, the children behaved more posi-

Figure 1.3

NAEYC ACCREDITATION CRITERIA: RECOMMENDED STAFF-CHILD RATIOS WITHIN GROUP SIZE

SIZE OF GROUP										
Age of Children / 6	8	10	12	14	16	18	20	22	24	28
Infants (birth–12 months) — 1:3	1:4									
Toddlers (12–24 months) — 1:3	1:4	1:5	1:4							
Two-year-olds (24–30 months) —	1:4	1:5	1:6							
Two and a half years old (30–36 months) —			1:6	1:7						
Three-year-olds —				1:7	1:8	1:9	1:10			
Four-year-olds —					1:8	1:9	1:10			
Five-year-olds —					1:8	1:9	1:10			
Six- to eight-year-olds —							1:10	1:11	1:12	
Nine- to twelve-year-olds —									1:12	1:14

Smaller group sizes and lower staff-child ratios have been found to be strong predictors of compliance with indicators of quality such as positive interactions among staff and children and developmentally appropriate curriculum. Variations in group sizes and ratios are acceptable only in cases where the program demonstrates a very high level of compliance with criteria for interactions, curriculum, staff qualifications, health and safety, and physical environment.

Source: B. Willer, "Estimating the Full Cost of Quality," in B. Willer, ed., *Reaching the Full Cost of Quality in Early Childhood Programs* (Washington, DC: National Association for the Education of Young Children, 1990), p. 64.

tively, were more cooperative, and were more involved in the program. These children also made the greatest gains on standardized tests of learning. In contrast, the National Child Care Staffing Study found that a college education was more important than specific early childhood training.[65]

HEALTH AND SAFETY

There has been a great deal of public concern about the transmission of illness in child care, but health risks in group programs can be reduced. One clear demarcation between early childhood programs in which children become ill often and those in which they do not is that when adults wash their hands frequently, children are healthier.[66] Children's safety also can be improved when providers are trained in maintaining a hazard-free environment.

RELATIONSHIP BETWEEN CAREGIVER
AND PARENTS

There is some evidence, albeit nonconclusive, from the longitudinal studies that when early childhood programs are effective, they do much more than teach the child. David Weikart states that one of the hallmarks of an effective program is that "teaching staff work with parents as partners in their children's development."[67] Lally and his colleagues at the Syracuse Family Development Research Program also attribute a great deal of the success of their model intervention program to parent partnerships:

> It seems clear that our original notion to involve parents as intervention agents paid off. One hypothesis that could be generated for the long-range differences between the samples is the lasting impact on the parent and the parent-child relationship after the intervention ceased.[68]

A conviction that parent partnerships pay off has led toward the development of "family-centered programming."[69]

Overall, research on the impact of child care programs on children's development shows connections between group size, staff-child ratios, health and safety, teacher training and education, and children's social, physical, and intellectual well-being. Contrary to the assumptions of some who argue that regulation will make child care more bureaucratic and less caring, good regulations seem to increase the likelihood of a more nurturing relationship. Again, good regulation does not by itself assure quality, but makes its existence more likely. For instance, teachers are more likely to be warm, caring, and stimulating when there is a good teacher-child ratio, when they understand children's normal development, and when the groups are not too large.

WHO IS AT RISK FROM LOW QUALITY?

Research on the benefits of early childhood education and care has concentrated on children from low socioeconomic backgrounds and has found that they, in fact, do benefit the most from quality programs. However, research on the detriments of poor-quality programs shows that higher socioeconomic background does not shield children from low-quality child care arrangements. Children, high- and low-income alike, have been shown to suffer ill effects when they are crowded in programs, when they receive little individualized attention, when they wander aimlessly about, or are pressured into inappropriate activities beyond their grasp. A recent study by Howes, Shinn, Sakai, Phillips, Galinsky, and Whitebook showed that even strong family circumstances could not buffer a child from the impact of low-quality child care.[70] In poor settings, children have a reduced capacity to learn how to learn, to care about learning, to feel competent, or to see the world as a place worth learning about.

States tend to target programs for so-called "at-risk" children (usually defined as at risk for dropping out of high school) for three key reasons. First, research has pinpointed low-income children as gaining the most from early childhood intervention programs. Second, middle-income families already tend to use early childhood programs. Third, state budget constraints limit funds available for these programs. The National Education Goals support this practice by stating: "All disadvantaged and disabled children" should "have access to high-quality and developmentally appropriate preschool programs."[71]

However, the National Child Care Staffing Study found that middle-income children are in the poorest-quality center-based programs with the worst staff-child ratios, least trained staff, least developmentally appropriate activities, and highest staff turnover. As a result, policy makers should be careful not to define quality as an issue solely for children from low-income families.[72]

There are other reasons that argue against targeting child care policies toward low-income children alone. First, labeling children may be harmful. Across the country, "at-risk" classes are known by that epithet by their teachers and their parents, and this can lead to stereotyping and self-fulfilling prophecies of failure. Second, such a policy may create de facto segregation. "At-risk" children are disproportionately minority, and the unintended consequence of such policies in some communities has been the creation of segregated child care programs. Third, children learn best within a diverse group. Young children from language-poor environments can prosper by being with children who enjoy talking, reading, and expressing themselves, and children from language-rich environments can learn a range of social, physical, creative, and cultural skills by interacting with others.

REFERENCES

1. S. L. Hofferth, A Brayfield, S. Deitch, and P. Holcomb, *The National Child Care Survey* (Washington, DC: The Urban Institute, 1991).

2. Committee for Economic Development, *The Unfinished Agenda: A New Vision for Child Development and Education* (New York: CED, 1991), p. 10.

3. W. B. Johnston and A. H. Packer, *Workforce 2000* (Indianapolis: Hudson Institute, 1987).

4. W. B. Johnston and A. H. Packer, 1987.

5. U.S. Bureau of Labor Statistics, *Labor Force Activity of Mothers of Young Children Continues at Record Pace*, News release 85-381 (Washington, DC: U.S. Department of Labor, September 19, 1985).

6. U.S. Bureau of Labor Statistics, unpublished data, 1990.

7. W. B. Johnston and A. H. Packer, 1987.

8. U.S. Bureau of Labor Statistics, 1990.

9. U.S. Bureau of Labor Statistics, 1990.

10. B. Willer, S. L. Hofferth, E. E. Kisker, P. D. Hawkins, E. Farquhar, and F. B. Glanz, *The Demand and Supply of Child Care in 1990* (Washington, DC: National Association for the Education of Young Children; U.S. Department of Health and Human Services, Administration on Children, Youth, and Families; U.S. Department of Education, Office of the Undersecretary, 1991).

11. E. Galinsky, D. E. Friedman, and C. A. Hernandez, *The Corporate Reference Guide to Work-Family Programs* (New York: Families and Work Institute, 1991).

12. J. T. Bond, E. Galinsky, M. Lord, G. L. Staines, and K. R. Brown, *Beyond the Parental Leave Debate: The Impact of Laws in Four States* (New York: Families and Work Institute, 1991).

13. W. B. Johnston and A. H. Packer, 1987.

14. Rodgers and Associates, "At a Crossroads: Women in Corporate America in the 1990s," paper prepared for the Ford Foundation (Boston: Rodgers and Associates, 1990).

15. *The Corporate Woman Officer* (Chicago: Heidrich and Struggles, Inc., 1986).

16. *Korn/Ferry International's Executive Profile: Corporate Leaders in the Eighties* (CA: Korn/Ferry International, 1986).

17. F. Schwartz, "Women in the Corporation: Where Are They?" Speech given at The Conference Board conference, New York City, Women in the Corporation: The Value-Added, May, 1988.

18. W. B. Johnston and A. H. Packer, 1987.

19. S. L. Hofferth et al., 1991.

20. S. L. Hofferth et al., 1991.

21. S. L. Hofferth et al., 1991.

22. S. L. Hofferth et al., 1991.

23. S. L. Hofferth, "Demand for and Supply of Child Care in the U.S." *Young Children* (July 1989).

24. E. Lindner Mattis and J. Rogers, *When the Churches Mind the Children* (New York: National Council of Churches, 1983).

25. E. E. Kisker, S. L. Hofferth, D. A. Phillips, and E. Farquhar, *A Profile of Child Care Settings: Early Education and Care in 1990*, Vol. 1 (Princeton: Mathematica Policy Research, Inc., 1991).

26. E. Galinsky et al., 1991.

27. E. E. Kisker et al., 1991.

28. S. L. Hofferth et al., 1991.

29. E. E. Kisker et al., 1991.

30. U.S. Congress, *Congressional Quarterly Weekly Report, November 3, 1990*, Vol. 48, No. 44, pp. 3721–3770 (Washington, DC: GPO, 1990).

31. C. D. Hayes, J. L. Palmer, and M. S. Zaslow, eds., *Child Care*, HRD-90-26HR (Washington, DC: GPO, 1990).

32. E. Galinsky, "The Role of the Corporation in Promoting Early Childhood Education and Care and Family Support Systems," in D. A. Steglin, ed., *Early Childhood Education: Policy Issues for the 1990s* (Norwood, NJ: Ablex Publishing Corp., in press).

33. E. E. Kisker et al., 1991.

34. K. Dickenson, "Child Care," in G. Duncan and J. Morgan, eds. *Five Thousand American Families, Patterns of Economic Progress*, Vol. III (Ann Arbor, MI: Institute for Social Research, 1975).

35. G. Duncan and C. R. Hill, "Model Choice in Child Care Arrangements," in G. Duncan and J. Morgan, eds. *Five Thousand American Families, Patterns of Economic Progress*, Vol. III (Ann Arbor, MI: Institute for Social Research, 1975).

36. J. Morgan, "Child Care When Parents Are Employed," in M. Hill, D. Hill, and J. Morgan, eds., *Five Thousand American Families, Patterns of Economic Progress*, Vol. IX (Ann Arbor, MI: Institute for Social Research, 1981).

37. M. Kurz, P. K. Robins, and R. G. Spiegelman, *A Study of the Demand for Child Care by Working Mothers* (Menlo Park, CA: Stanford Research Institute, 1975).

38. R. Shortlidge and P. Brito, *How Women Arrange for the Care of Their Children While They Work: A Study of Child Care Arrangements, Costs, and Preference in 1971* (Columbus, OH: Center for Human Resource Research, 1971).

39. W. Gray, "Latchkey Children: Unlocking the Door to School-Age Child Care," Ph.D. Dissertation, Brandeis University, 1985.

40. S. L. Hofferth et al., 1991.

41. S. Bredekamp, ed., *Accreditation Criteria and Procedures for the National Academy of Early Childhood Programs* (Washington, DC: National Association for the Education of Young Children, 1984).

42. C. D. Hayes et al., 1990.

43. T. J. Gamble and E. Zigler, "Effects of Infant Day Care: Another Look at the Evidence," *American Journal of Orthopsychiatry*, Vol. 56, No. 1 (January 1986), pp. 26–42.

44. C. Howes, C. Rodning, D. C. Galluzzo, and L. Myers, "Attachment and Child Care: Relationships with Mother and Caregiver," *Early Childhood Research Quarterly*, Vol. 3, No. 4, December 1988, pp. 403–416.

45. D. Phillips, K. McCartney, and S. Scarr, "Child Care Quality and Children's Social Development, *Developmental Psychology*, Vol. 23 (1987), pp. 537–543.

46. K. McCartney, "The Effect of Quality of Day Care Environment upon Children's Language Development," *Developmental Psychology*, Vol. 20 (1984), pp. 244–260.

47. D. P. Weikart, Testimony at the U.S. Congressional Subcommittee on Education and Health, Joint Economic Committee, February 26, 1990, p. 4.

48. M. Whitebook, C. Howes, and D. A. Phillips, *Who Cares? Child Care Teachers and the Quality of Care in America, Final Report. National Child Care Staffing Study* (Oakland, CA: Child Care Employee Project, 1990).

49. D. L. Vandell, K. Henderson, and K. S. Wilson, "A Longitudinal Study of Children with Varying Day Care Experiences," *Child Development*, Vol. 59 (1988), pp. 1286–1292.

50. D. Elkind, *Miseducation: Preschoolers at Risk* (New York: Alfred A. Knopf, 1987).

51. D. L. Vandell and C. P. Powers, "Day Care Quality and Children's Free Play Activities," *American Journal of Orthopsychiatry*, Vol. 53, No. 3 (1983), pp. 493–500.

52. R. A. Arend, F. L. Gove, and L. A. Stroufe, "Continuity of Individual Adaptation from Infancy to Kindergarten: A Predictive Study of Ego-Resiliency and Curiosity in Preschoolers," *Child Development*, Vol. 59 (1979), pp. 950–959.

53. E. A. Farber and B. Egeland, "Developmental Consequences of Out-of-Home Care for Infants in Low-Income Population," in E. F. Zigler and E. W. Gordon, eds., *Day Care: Scientific and Social Policy Issues* (Boston: Auburn House, 1982), pp. 102–125.

54. S. Londerville and M. Main, "Security of Attachment, Compliance, and Maternal Training Methods in the Second Year of Life," *Developmental Psychology*, Vol. 17, No. 3 (1981), pp. 289–299.

55. N. W. Finkelstein, "Aggression: Is it Stimulated by Day Care?" *Young Children*, Vol. 37, No. 6 (1982), p. 8.

56. N. W. Finkelstein, 1982.

57. E. M. Cummings, *Caregiver Stability in Day Care: Continuity vs. Daily Association*, paper presented at the International Conference on Infant Studies, Los Angeles, April 1986.

58. C. Howes and P. Stewart, "Child's Play with Adults, Toys and Peers: An Examination of Family and Child Care Influences," *Developmental Psychology*, Vol. 23 (1987), pp. 423–430.

59. M. Whitebook et al., 1990.

60. R. R. Ruopp, J. Travers, F. Glanz, and Craig Coelen, *Children at the Center: Final Report of the National Day Care Study*, Vol. 1 (Cambridge, MA: Abt Associates, 1979).

61. M. Whitebook et al., 1990.

62. P. Divine-Hawkins, *National Day Care Home Study: Family Day Care in the United States* (Washington, DC: 1981).

63. D. Howes and J. Rubenstein, "Determinants of Toddlers' Experience in Day Care: Age of Entry and Quality of Setting," *Child Care Quarterly* Vol. 14, No. 2 (1985), pp. 140–151.

64. R. R. Ruopp et al., 1979.

65. M. Whitebook et al., 1990.

66. S. Aronson, "Maintaining Health in Child Care Settings," in B. M. Caldwell, ed., *Group Care for Young Children: A Supplement to Parental Care, Proceedings of the Twelfth Johnson & Johnson Pediatric Round Table* (Lexington, MA: Lexington Books, 1987), pp. 163–172.

67. D. P. Weikart, 1990, p. 6.

68. J. R. Lally, P. L. Mangione, and A. S. Honig, *The Syracuse University Family Development Research Program: Long Range Impact of Early Intervention on Low-Income Children and Their Families* (Syracuse, NY: Syracuse University Family Research Program, 1987).

69. E. Galinsky and B. Weissbourd, *Family-Centered Child Care*, in *Yearbook in Early Childhood Education*, B. Spodek and O. Saracho, eds. Volume 3 (New York: Teachers College Press, 1992), pp. 47–65.

70. C. Howes, M. Shinn, L. M. Sakai, D. Phillips, E. Galinsky, and M. Whitebook, *Race, Social Class, and Maternal Working Conditions* *as Influences on Children's Development in Child Care* (Los Angeles: UCLA, in preparation).

71. National Governors' Association, "National Education Goals" (Washington, DC: National Governors' Association, February 25, 1990).

72. M. Whitebook et al., 1990.

CHAPTER 2

Child Care Problems: How Is the System Working Now?

We are a long way off from being able to deliver the kind of quality outlined in the last chapter to most children. Providing this kind of high quality is expensive and requires a trade-off. Higher quality means higher cost and could possibly mean fewer choices for consumers, due to diminishing supply, and the pricing of some consumers out of the market altogether. On the other hand, very low-quality care can damage a child's development, regardless of his or her social class, and may also incur societal costs later on — whether in the form of additional remedial education or welfare transfers.

Quality and related cost questions, however, are not the only problems afflicting our child care system. Even without striving for the kind of high quality outlined in the last chapter, there are major problems with our nation's child care system — one that is not really a system as much as a patchwork of uncoordinated arrangements: It is difficult for parents to find child care or information on child care options. There is high turnover among child care providers because of very low wages and poor working conditions. In addition, it is difficult to enforce regulations on even a minimum floor of quality. This chapter outlines some of these problems.

SUPPLY–DEMAND GAPS

In 1990, there were an estimated 80,000 centers in operation serving between 4 and 5.1 million children. Between 1976 and 1990, the number of center-based programs tripled, and the number of children cared for in these programs quadrupled, with much of this increase coming from serving increasingly younger children. The proportion of children under three in centers doubled between 1976 and 1990.[1] In 1990, there also were 118,000 regulated family child care homes, serving approximately 700,000 children and an estimated 685,000 to 1.2 million nonregulated family child care providers for 3.4 million children.[2] Are these arrangements enough to meet demand?

In general, the public believes that there is not enough child care. It takes parents five weeks on average to find child care, while it takes child care centers eight days on average to fill a vacancy, a regulated family child care provider 25 days to do so, and a nonregulated provider 23 days.[3] A study of employee child care needs conducted by a large pharmaceutical firm in the Northeast found that half of all parents reported some or great difficulty in finding care, 79 percent reported difficulty when looking for care for mildly sick children, 60 percent found it difficult to find infant care, and 54 percent reported difficulty in locating school-age care. The lowest percentage, 39 percent, indicated that it was difficult to find child care for preschoolers.[4]

In a 1987 survey by the American Federation of State, County, and Municipal Employees (AFSCME), more than half of a nationally representative sample thought the supply of child care was inadequate, while only one quarter thought it was adequate.[5] The problem is particularly acute for center-based care. The Profile of Child Care Settings Study, conducted for the Department of Education by Mathematica Policy Research (one of the first studies to include all forms of education and care facilities) found that centers are filled to an average of 88 percent capacity, a rate "sufficiently high to suggest that the supply of care in center-based early childhood programs is close to being utilized fully."[6] In addition, between two thirds and three fourths of centers reported having no vacancies. When the Profile of Child Care Settings Study looked at all care for children under the age of two, it found that fewer than 10 percent of centers had vacancies for infants, fewer than 16 percent had vacancies for one-year-olds, and fewer than 30 percent had vacancies for two-year-olds.[7]

Not only is care difficult to find, but parents are not always truly satisfied with the arrangement they use. For the most part, parents report that they are satisfied. In one study of center users in Atlanta, Georgia, 95 percent reported being satisfied. However, when these mothers were asked if they would select the program they were currently using again if other options were available, 53 percent said no, a significant number given how difficult it is for parents to admit that their child is in a less than optimal situation.[8]

Studies have found that parental satisfaction varies with the type of arrangement. A Portland, Oregon, study found that 57 percent of the parents using care by their own children (self-care or latchkey care) reported some degree of dissatisfaction, as compared to 23 percent using centers or family child care.[9]

Meanwhile, the demand for child care has been increasing. During the 1980s, the number of preschoolers increased, as did the labor force participation of mothers. While the size of the preschool population may not rise significantly during the 1990s, 40 percent more preschoolers may need child care because their mothers are more likely to work.[10] Of the 22 million children under the age of six, about half have working mothers. Sandra Hofferth and Deborah Phillips predict that if trends continue to go as they were between 1970 and 1985, by 1995, two thirds of children, or just under 15 million preschoolers, will have employed mothers.[11]

These estimates do not incorporate the impact of the 1988 Family Support Act that requires mothers receiving public assistance to seek employment if their children are older than three years old (or over one year old, if a state so chooses). These welfare mothers are expected to swell the ranks of child care seekers with low-level skills and low wages.

Of the 7.4 million children under age five who are the youngest among their siblings and whose mothers worked in 1990, 47 percent were in the care of relatives (28 percent cared for by parents, and 19 percent cared for by other relatives, predominantly grandparents, in the child's home or the relative's home). Another 3 percent relied on a nonrelative in the child's home. The remaining 48 percent used out-of-home, nonrelative care. In this latter figure, 20 percent used family child care (both licensed and unlicensed) where a neighbor usually cared for the child in his or her own home, and 28 percent used a child care center, pre-school, or nursery school.[12]

These rates of use indicate a decline between 1965 and 1990 in all forms of relative care (from 62 to 47 percent) and an increase in all forms of nonrelative care (from 37 to 51 percent) for the youngest preschool child (see Figure 2.1). A more detailed breakdown of these trends (see Figure 2.2) shows a considerable drop in care by relatives other than parents (from 33 to 19 percent), and by in-home providers or "sitter" care in the home (from 15 to 3 percent); a small increase in family child care home usage (from 16 to 20 percent); and dramatic increases in center-based care (from 6 to 28 percent).[13]

Concurrently, there has been a rapid increase in public school enrollments for preschool children with both em-ployed and at-home mothers. Of mothers whose youngest child is under five years old, the proportion of three- and four-year-old children in prekindergarten programs is 51 percent, and the number of five-year-olds in kindergarten, both public and private, is 90 percent.[14] Middle-class chil-dren are much more likely to attend a school program, pub-lic or private, than low-income children.[15]

In the public's mind, many low-income children are in Head Start, but it serves only an estimated 25 to 33 percent of the eligible three-, four-, and five-year-olds.[16] However, an estimated 70 percent of Head Start–eligible five-year-olds attend some type of public or private program.[17] Thus we can assume that a more accurate figure for eligible chil-dren served by Head Start is closer to 25 to 30 percent. This is expected to increase, as Congress has passed legislation for full funding of Head Start by 1994 and as the Clinton administration has expressed a commitment to expanding Head Start.[18] Head Start parents are increasingly em-

Figure 2.1

CHANGES IN PRIMARY CHILD CARE ARRANGEMENTS FOR YOUNGEST CHILDREN UNDER FIVE WITH EMPLOYED MOTHERS

1965–1990

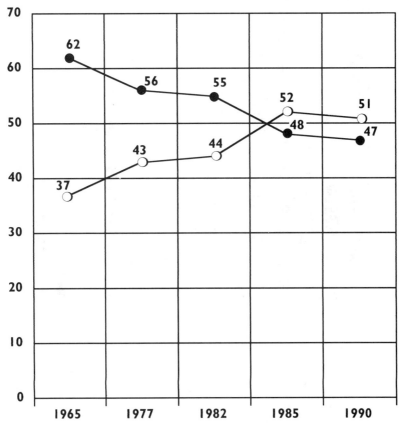

Percent

- ●— Relative (Parents and other relatives)
- ○— Non-Relative (In-home care, family child care, centers)

Source: Adapted from U.S. Census Bureau, 1965–1985; S. L. Hofferth, A. Brayfield, S. Deitch, and P. Holcomb, *The National Child Care Survey, 1990* (Washington, DC: The Urban Institute, 1991).

43

Figure 2.2

PRIMARY CARE FOR THE YOUNGEST PRESCHOOL CHILD WITH EMPLOYED MOTHERS

1965–1990

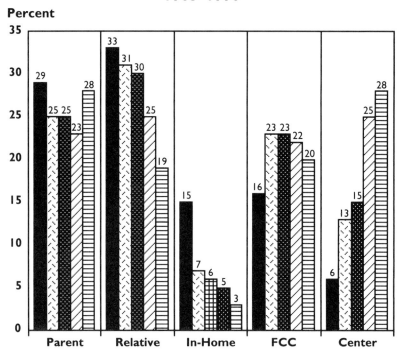

CHILD CARE ARRANGEMENT

Source: S. L. Hofferth, A. Brayfield, S. Deitch, and P. Holcomb, *The National Child Care Survey, 1990* (Washington, DC: The Urban Institute, 1991), p. 99.

ployed. The National Head Start Association estimates that 32 percent of Head Start parents work full-time and 19 percent work part-time, yet only 6 percent of Head Start programs are full-day (over nine hours a day).[19] When Head Start parents were asked to rate areas that needed improvement and expansion, they were most likely to request full-day services.[20]

THE STAFFING CRISIS

As mentioned in the last chapter, a stable relationship between caregiver and child is a critical ingredient in providing high-quality care. Children have an easier time separating from their parents when they know their caregivers, and the National Child Care Staffing Study found that children in programs with high staff turnover achieved less in social and language development.

Unfortunately, high staff turnover in the child care profession is currently one of the largest problems. In addition, fewer workers are willing to enter the child care field.

A decline in the population of eighteen- to twenty-four-year-olds—prime years for child care workers—is partly responsible for these staffing problems, as are labor shortages in other service industries. The field has become less attractive to young people who have other employment opportunities that offer better pay, more respect, and no fingerprint checks. A constant flow of replacements is needed to offset high levels of turnover among child care providers. An estimated 60 percent of family child care providers and 41 percent of teachers, assistant teachers, and teaching aides in centers leave the field each year.[21] The Profile of Child Care Settings Study found a national turnover rate of 25 percent for teachers (not including assistant teachers and aides) across all types of early childhood programs.[22]

At a meeting of child care experts, Jerlean Daniel, the director of a Pittsburgh center, described the extent of the staffing crisis.

> I know how to provide a high-quality program, but what I've only been able to admit in public recently is that there is no way I can really do it. How can I provide a quality program if I can't find teachers? How can I provide a quality program if I can't find substitutes? How can I provide a quality program if those of us who remain in the center are burned out?[23]

The National Child Care Staffing Study, a comprehensive study of 227 randomly selected centers in five cities, set out to explain the high turnover rates and teacher shortages crippling child care centers across the country. Not surprisingly, teachers' wages were one of the most important predictors of children's development and teacher retention.[24]

According to the Staffing Study, most staff in child care centers were women under the age of forty. While less than half of the women in the total U.S. labor force have attended college, more than half of the assistant teachers and almost three quarters of the teachers in child care programs had some college background. (Many states do not require teachers in child care programs to have college degrees; some only require them to be over eighteen years old.) Despite these staff attributes, the average 1988 hourly wage in a child care center was $5.35, which amounts to $9,363 per year. The 1988 poverty threshold for a family of four was $9,431. Forty-two percent of these teachers, assistant teachers, and aides earned at least half of their household income, and one quarter earned over two thirds of it. It is not surprising that 25 percent of full-time staff found it necessary to work a second job.

Another study, the Profile of Child Care Settings Study, conducted for the Department of Education by Mathematica Policy Research, also examined national data on teacher training and education. It found that 93 percent of teachers (not including assistant teachers and aides) have some specialized early childhood education training, the most common form of which is attendance at child care workshops or courses. It also found that teachers in early childhood education and care programs are relatively well educated. Forty-seven percent of center-based teachers have a college degree, 13 percent have a two-year college degree, and 14 percent ended their formal education after high school.[25]

The Profile of Child Care Settings Study also investigated the issue of wages for a national sample of early childhood teachers (not including teaching assistants and aides). This study found that the annual salary for a preschool teacher in a center was $11,500 in 1990. However, half of all teachers earned less than $11,000. Teachers in full-day programs earned an average of $6.84 an hour, $5.43 in for-profit programs, and $14.40 in public-school-based programs.[26]

When comparing the findings from both of these studies to a similar one conducted in 1977, one can see gains in teachers' formal education and experience, but a striking decline in salaries. According to the Staffing Study, teachers' salaries, when adjusted for inflation, dropped by 27 percent, assistants' pay dropped by 20 percent, and child care staff earned significantly less than comparably educated men and women.[27] (See Figure 2.3.) The Staffing

47

Figure 2.3
EDUCATIONAL LEVELS

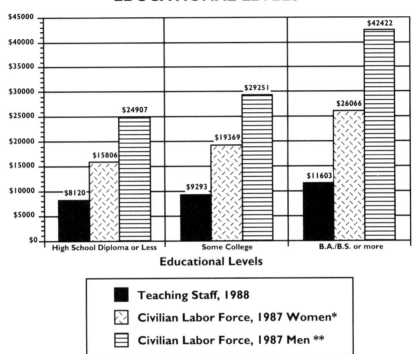

Educational Levels

Teaching Staff, 1988

Civilian Labor Force, 1987 Women*

Civilian Labor Force, 1987 Men **

[a]Full-time annual; earnings based on 35 hours per week/50 weeks per year.

[b]1988 data not available.

Source: M. Whitebook, C. Howes, and D. A. Phillips, *Who Cares? Child Care Teachers and the Quality of Care in America, Final Report. National Child Care Staffing Study* (Oakland: Child Care Employee Project, 1990), p. 51.

Study also found, not surprisingly, that staff turnover was highest for teaching staff who earned the lowest wages.[28] (See Figure 2.4.)

A critical finding of both the Staffing Study and the Profile of Child Care Settings Study was the importance that program auspices played in the level of teacher turnover (see

Figure 2.4
SIX-MONTH TURNOVER RATES FOR TEACHING STAFF BY WAGES

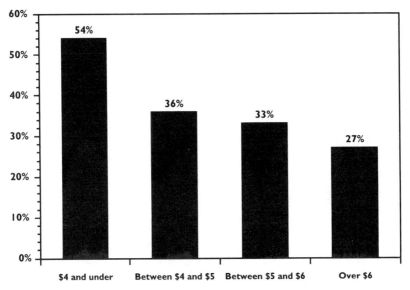

Source: M. Whitebook, C. Howes, and D. A. Phillips, *Who Cares? Child Care Teachers and the Quality of Care in America, Final Report. National Child Care Staffing Study* (Oakland: Child Care Employee Project, 1990), p. 75.

Figure 2.5). In the Staffing Study, nonprofit centers had a turnover rate of 30 percent and church-based centers 36 percent. Independent for-profit centers had a 56 percent turnover rate and for-profit centers functioning as part of a chain experienced turnover at the rate of 70 percent. Both types of nonprofit centers spent a higher proportion of their budgets on teaching staff than did for-profits (62 and 63 percent compared to 49 percent for independent for-profits and 41 percent for chains).[29]

Figure 2.5

ANNUAL TEACHER TURNOVER IN CENTERS[a]

Type of Program	Percentage of Programs That Experienced Teacher Turnover[b]	Average Teacher Turnover[b] in Programs with Turnover	Average Teacher Turnover[b] in All Programs
All Programs	50%	50%	25%
Nonprofit Programs			
Head Start Programs	31	64	20
Public-school-based programs	23	60	14
Religious-sponsored programs	54	41	23
Other sponsored programs	53	47	25
Independent programs	52	48	25
For-Profit Programs			
Chain programs	77	50	39
Independent programs	50	53	27
Samples Size	**1,773**	**832**	**1,773**

[a] Excludes programs that serve primarily handicapped children and programs that do not serve preschool children age three and above.

[b] Teacher turnover is defined as the number of teachers who left the program during the past twelve months divided by the total number of teachers employed by the program. This measure does not include assistant teachers and aides.

Source: E. E. Kisker, S. L. Hofferth, D. A. Phillips, and E. Farquhar, *A Profile of Child Care Settings, Early Education and Care in 1990*, Vol. I (Princeton: Mathematica Policy Research, Inc., 1991), p. 146.

THE DIFFICULTY OF REGULATING QUALITY

In this country, state licensing regulations are intended to set a floor of protection for children, though some states do have standards that promote high quality rather than a minimum floor of safety. Unfortunately, the types of care to be regulated vary widely state by state. All states regulate center care, but 13 states exempt church-run programs, and 22 states exempt part-day programs. Programs under the jurisdiction of state departments of education and federal agencies are exempt from state child care licensing laws in most states.

While most states regulate family child care homes that receive public funds, and almost all states have some regulatory mechanisms in place for some homes, 22 states exempt family child care homes that serve five or fewer unrelated children, and 36 states exempt those serving three or fewer unrelated children. Furthermore, according to the National Research Council, even where regulations, licensing requirements, and registration or certification provisions are in effect, enforcement is generally quite lax.[30, 31]

Regulating Group Size and Staff-Child Ratio

As mentioned in the last chapter, the relationship between the child and the teacher-caregiver is the factor that most affects children's development, but the presence of some licensing regulations makes a positive relationship much more likely:[32] the number of children allowed in a group (group size), the number of children per teacher (staff-child ratio), and teacher-caregiver education and training.

All states, including the District of Columbia, specify staff-child ratios for child care centers, but 25 have no group size requirements for infants and toddlers, and five have none for preschoolers. Sixteen states require no training for child care teachers in centers, and 40 have no training requirements for family child care providers.

Research shows that one adult should care for and teach no more than three to four infants, but 20 states have regulations that do not meet this standard. In fact, five states permit seven or more infants for every adult, and one midwestern state even permits a family child care provider to care for 15 infants. According to a recent review of state standards, the median of state standards is close to recommended standards, but "the variability across the states extends into a range of quality that may pose a risk to children."[33]

The Profile of Child Care Settings Study provides the first national picture of how state standards compare to quality standards in both center-based and regulated family child care. Quality standards are defined as the standards set for program accreditation by the National Association for the Education of Young Children (NAEYC) (see Chapter 1) and the standards that were agreed to by the federal government in 1980 but never put into law: the Health, Education, and Welfare Day Care Regulations (HEWDCR). In examining group size in center-based programs, the researchers concluded that care for children over age three is typically better than for children under three.[34] (See Figure 2.6.) The Profile of Child Care Settings Study also revealed that many programs for infants and toddlers fail to meet professionally agreed upon standards for staff-child ratios.[35] (See Figure 2.7.)

As Figures 2.6 and 2.7 indicate, a number of programs do not even meet their own state standards for group size or staff-child ratios, often because of the difficulties of enforc-

Figure 2.6

PERCENTAGE OF CENTERS THAT MEET PROFESSIONAL RECOMMENDATIONS[a] FOR AVERAGE GROUP SIZES

Age of Children	State Regulations[b]	NAEYC	HEWDCR[c]
0–5 months	73–100%	55–87%	32–67%
6–11 months	83–85	68–65	50–40
12–17 months	72–83	75–79	26–34
18–23 months	79–79	71–74	16–24
24–29 months	81–81	63–68[d]	63–68[d]
30–35 months	65–86	47–64[d]	47–64[d]
36–47 months	82–84	83–84	73–76
48–59 months	88–86	81–80	66–65
60–71 months	84–94	72–83	65–73
72–95 months	87–92	62–76	47–60
96 + months	95–79	71–51	64–44
Samples Sizes	**36–709**	**90–1,288**	**90–1,288**

[a] Ranges of percentages of programs that meet the group size recommendations are given. The first number is the percentage of programs meeting recommendations when groups are categorized by the age of the youngest child in the group (the method used in approximately half of the states in the sample). The second number is the percentage of programs that meet the recommendations when groups are categorized by the midpoint of the age range of children in the group. The second number is sometimes less than the first number because some groups fall into different age categories when the midpoint age is used.

[b] Includes only programs located in states with group size regulations.

[c] Health, Education, and Welfare Day Care Regulations promulgated in 1980, but never passed into law.

[d] The NAEYC and HEWDCR group size benchmarks are the same for these age groups.

Source: E. E. Kisker, S. L. Hofferth, D. A. Phillips, and E. Farquhar, *A Profile of Child Care Settings, Early Education and Care in 1990*, Vol. 1 (Princeton: Mathematica Policy Research, Inc., 1991), p. 121.

Note: The table reads: For groups in which *the youngest child* is zero to five months old, 73 percent of centers meet their state's group size regulation, 55 percent meet the NAEYC group size requirement, and 32 percent meet the HEWDCR group size requirement. If groups are categorized by the age of *the average child*, 100 percent of centers meet their state's group size regulatory for children zero to five months old, 87 percent meet the NAEYC group size criterion, and 67 percent meet the HEWDCR group size requirement.

Figure 2.7

PERCENTAGE OF CENTERS THAT MEET PROFESSIONAL RECOMMENDATIONS[a] FOR AVERAGE STAFF-CHILD RATIOS

Age of Children	State Regulations[b]	NAEYC	HEWDCR
0–5 months	82–92%	58–84%	28–56%
6–11 months	83–88	65–62	40–31
12–17 months	67–80	50–63	15–25
18–23 months	68–81	41–49	11–15
24–29 months	80–81	43–49	17–22
30–35 months	71–84	37–45	13–16
36–47 months	83–85	75–76	61–63
48–59 months	88–88	68–70	52–55
60–71 months	88–91	56–65	45–52
72–95 months	91–95	60–71	79–86
96+ months	95–91	58–53	86–82
Samples Sizes	**80–1,277**	**88–1,283**	**88–1,283**

[a] Ranges of percentages of programs that meet the group size recommendations are given. The first number is the percentage of programs meeting standards when groups are categorized by the age of the youngest child in the group (the method used in approximately half of the states in the sample). The second number is the percentage of programs that meet the standards when groups are categorized by the midpoint of the age range of children in the group. The second number is sometimes less than the first number because some groups fall into different age categories when the midpoint age is used.

[b] Includes only programs located in states with staff-child ratio regulations.

Source: E. E. Kisker, S. L. Hofferth, D. A. Phillips, and E. Farquhar, *A Profile of Child Care Settings, Early Education and Care in 1990*, Vol. I (Princeton: Mathematica Policy Research, Inc., 1991), p. 129.

Note: The table reads: For groups in which *the youngest child* is zero to five months old, 82 percent of centers meet their state's ratio regulation, 58 percent meet the NAEYC-recommended ratio, and 28 percent meet the HEWDCR group size requirement. If groups are categorized by the age of *the average child*, 92 percent of centers meet their state's ratio regulation, 84 percent meet the NAEYC ratio criterion, and 56 percent meet the HEWDCR ratio requirement.

ing standards: Licensing officials may be insufficiently trained or have impossibly high case loads. Furthermore, when there are budget cutbacks, the state's licensing capacity is often diminished. The programs that do not meet their own states' regulatory standards often fall far from them. For example, the centers that do not meet group size requirements maintain group sizes that are on average twice as large as their state laws specify. Likewise, the centers that fail to meet required staff-child ratios have, on average, twice as many children in the care of one adult than is mandated.[36]

These findings have led the researchers for the Department of Education study to conclude that since many programs for infants and toddlers exceed or are close to exceeding their state licensing requirements, "programs and parents may be accepting lower-quality care in order to make infant and toddler care financially viable."[37]

REFERENCES

1. E. E. Kisker, S. L. Hofferth, D. A. Phillips, and E. Farquhar, *A Profile of Child Care Settings, Early Education and Care in 1990*, Vol. 1 (Princeton: Mathematica Policy Research, Inc., 1991).

2. E. E. Kisker et al., 1991.

3. B. Willer, S. L. Hofferth, E. E. Kisker, P. Divine-Hawkins, E. Farquhar, and F. B. Glanz, *The Demand and Supply of Child Care in 1990* (Washington, DC: National Association for the Education of Young Children; U.S. Department of Health and Human Services, Administration on Children, Youth, and Families; U.S. Department of Education, Office of the Undersecretary, 1991).

4. E. Galinsky, *Child Care and Productivity* (New York: Families and Work Institute, 1988).

5. American Federation of State, County and Municipal Employees, AFL-CIO, *America's Child Care Needs, A 1987 AFSCME National Secretaries Week Opinion Poll* (Washington, DC: AFSCME, 1987).

6. E. E. Kisker et al., 1991.

7. E. E. Kisker et al., 1991.

8. M. Shinn, E. Galinsky, and L. Gulcur, *The Role of Child Care Centers in the Lives of Parents* (New York: Families and Work Institute, 1990).

9. A. C. Amlen and P. E. Koren, *Hard to Find and Difficult to Manage: The Effects of Child Care on the Workplace* (Portland, OR: Regional Research Institute for Human Services, Portland State University, 1984).

10. E. E. Kisker, R. Maynard, A. Gordon, and M. Strain, *The Child Care Challenge: What Parents Need and What Is Available in*

Three Metropolitan Areas, report prepared for U.S. Department of Health and Human Services (Princeton: Mathematica Policy Research, Inc., 1989).

11. S. L. Hofferth and D. A. Phillips, "Child Care in the United States, 1970–1995," *Journal of Marriage and the Family*, Vol. 49 (1987), pp. 559–571.

12. S. L. Hofferth, A. Brayfield, S. Deitch, and P. Holcomb, *The National Child Care Survey 1990* (Washington, DC: The Urban Institute Press, 1991).

13. S. L. Hofferth et al., 1991.

14. U.S. Bureau of the Census, *School Enrollment — Social and Economic Characteristics of Students: October 1985 and 1984*, Current Population Reports, Series P-20, No. 426 (Washington, DC: GPO, 1988).

15. A. Kahn and S. B. Kamerman, *Child Care: Facing the Hard Choices* (Dover, MA: Auburn House, 1987).

16. Congressional Research Services, *Head Start Program: Background Information and Issues* (Washington, DC: GPO, 1990).

17. U.S. House of Representatives, Committee on Education and Labor, *Report on the Human Services Reorganization Act of 1990*, (Washington, DC: GPO, 1990), p. 29.

18. J. Lombardi, personal communication, October 1990.

19. National Head Start Association, Testimony of Eugenia Boggus, President of NHSA, before the House Committee on Education and Labor, March 6, 1989 (Washington, DC: Congressional Research Services, 1990).

20. J. Lombardi, *Head Start: The Nation's Pride, A Nation's Challenge*, Final Report. Silver Ribbon Panel (Alexandria, VA: National Head Start Association, 1990).

21. E. Galinsky, 1988, M. Whitebook, C. Howes, and D. A. Phillips, *Who Cares? Child Care Teachers and the Quality of Care in America*, Final Report, National Child Care Staffing Study (Oakland, CA: Child Care Employee Project, 1990).

22. E. E. Kisker et al., 1991.

23. J. Daniel, personal communication, 1989.

24. M. Whitebook et al., 1990.

25. E. E. Kisker et al., 1991.

26. E. E. Kisker et al., 1991.

27. M. Whitebook et al., 1990.

28. M. Whitebook et al., 1990.

29. M. Whitebook et al., 1990.

30. C. G. Adams, *Who Knows How Safe? The Status of State Efforts to Ensure Quality Child Care* (Washington, DC: Children's Defense Fund, 1990).

31. C. D. Hayes, J. L. Palmer, and M. J. Zaslow, eds., *Who Cares for America's Children? Child Care Policy for the 1990s* (Washington, DC: National Academy Press, 1990).

32. M. Whitebook et al., 1990.

33. D. Phillips, J. Lande, and Marc Goldberg, "The State of Child Care Regulation: A Comparative Analysis," *Early Childhood Research Quarterly*, Vol. 5, No. 2 (June 1990), pp. 151–179.

34. E. E. Kisker et al., 1991.

35. E. E. Kisker et al., 1991.

36. E. E. Kisker et al., 1991.

37. E. E. Kisker et al., 1991, p. 125.

CHAPTER 3

The Benefits of Typical and High-Quality Child Care

C hildren, parents, business, and society all have different demands of child care, and all can reap different benefits from it. Children can make developmental gains. Working parents can reduce or eliminate the stress they experience when they rely on low-quality care or a patchwork of different care arrangements. Parents with fewer child care breakdowns miss fewer days of work, arrive late and leave early less often, and have fewer worries or distractions while on the job — all of which reap gains for their employers. In addition, companies that help their employees with child care — whether through an on-site center, resource and referral service, flexible scheduling, or other child care benefits — might be more successful at recruiting and retaining top talent. Finally, society may benefit from the developmental gains made by children in high-quality care, particularly low-income children. There is some evidence, though still inconclusive and controversial, that very high-quality early childhood programs for low-income children can reduce the likelihood of juvenile delinquency, special education, and welfare dependence — the costs of which society bears.

In any case, the potential for gains for society, children, parents, and business is significant enough to warrant further study of the costs and benefits of quality and to urge policy makers and business to deal with quality and affordability issues.

BENEFITS FOR BUSINESS AND PARENTS
Absenteeism Rates

Companies expect a certain amount of absenteeism from their employees, and most recognize that some absence is healthy — for example, to provide a temporary release from stress. Several studies suggest that rigid efforts to ensure perfect attendance may lead to unintended and negative consequences, such as reduced product quality and increased accidents.[1] At the same time, companies have begun to realize that while some absences are inevitable (e.g., for serious illness in the family), some can be avoided (e.g., for a mildly sick child or a child care breakdown), if supportive programs are available.

Medium-sized and large companies offer one form or another of sick leave, vacation or disability leave, and personal days, thus designating legitimate reasons for absence. According to the 1990 Families and Work study of 188 large companies, 16 percent allowed employees to take a leave of absence specifically for family-related reasons.[2]

The average worker loses between seven and nine days a

year, and 52 percent of absences for parents are due to family problems.[3,4] Family-related absences are influenced by:

- Presence, number, and age of children

- Marital status

- Gender

- Form of child care used

- Occupational level

- Family income

- Company policies

Arthur Emlen of Portland State University details the family reasons for absence as follows:

> If the work force misses about nine days per
> year, men who have no children miss 7.5 days.
> Add a half a day for being a father, one day for
> using out-of-home care, or 5.5 days if the
> children look after themselves. This brings the
> total for men to 13.5 days. Women without
> children start at 9.5 days absent. Two days can
> be added if kids are in care outside the home or
> 3.5 days if they look after themselves. Add
> another three days if she is a single parent. If
> she is in management, she will miss a day or two
> less, but she will be late to work most often since

her job will allow it. Having a family income of $30,000 or more saves women in management and professional positions nearly two days or a half day for women who are not in that position. The income difference saves men one day at either occupational level. Take off several days if the company's personnel policies severely clamp down on absenteeism, but add stress.[5]

Various studies show that levels of absenteeism and stress differ, depending on the employee's child caring responsibilities. Causes of absenteeism include the need to care for a sick child, trouble finding child care, and breakdowns of child care arrangements.

INCOME AND GENDER DIFFERENCES

Reports conflict as to whether low-income or better-paid employees experience higher rates of absenteeism. Ellen Galinsky cites one study that found that lower-paid employees, particularly men, are more likely than those who are better paid to have child care–related absences.[6] But studies repeatedly confirm that absenteeism is related less to gender than to the worker's economic status within the family and responsibility for caring for children. Emlen and Koren found in a Portland, Oregon, study of 8,000 employees that in two-earner families, women missed 50 percent more days per year than men.[7] Since women tend to earn less than men, having the woman stay home to cope with family emergencies is a rational economic decision.

While men miss work due to child care problems less frequently than women, when they do miss work because of child care, they are more likely to have higher levels of stress as a result. This may be a function of informal norms, or sanctions against men who assume greater family responsibility.[8]

In addition, the Census Bureau reports that among full-time workers, women are more likely than men to have had one or more work interruptions lasting six months or longer. In 1984, 42 percent of full-time working women (compared to 12.1 percent of men) said they had at some time interrupted their work for a period of six months or longer. Of this 42 percent, 36 percent gave "family reasons" as the cause of the interruption.[9]

SICK CHILDREN

A study at Adolph Coors Company found sick child care problems to be the leading cause of absence.[10] The 55 parents at Coors, studied as a group, missed 230 days in a six-month period (460 days per year) due to child care problems. The reasons broke down as follows:

- 146 days (63 percent) due to sick children

- 65 days (28 percent) due to the search for child care

- 19 days (8 percent) due to a breakdown in child care

Children under the age of twelve are sick for an average of five days per year. According to the National Child Care Survey 1990, 35 percent of all employed mothers reported that they had sick children "in the last month," and 51 percent stayed home to care for these children.[11,12] In a *Fortune* magazine study of a nationally representative sample of two-earner families with children twelve years old and under, 57 percent of the respondents said that finding care for a sick child was a major problem.[13] Fernandez found that sick child care was at the top of a list of 15 possible child care problems. The problem was greater for women, who are far more likely than men to have to stay home with a sick child.[14]

Parents resort to a variety of strategies to take time off for a sick child. At one large hospital, 36 percent of parents took a day off without pay, another 30 percent took a personal sick day, and 24 percent took vacation days. In a 33-company study, half the parents took vacation days. Women were far more likely than men to take days without pay to care for a sick child (24 percent compared to 4 percent). Men were more likely than women to take personal sick days (24 percent compared to 13 percent).[16]

Whether a parent will stay home with a sick child depends on the severity of the illness, the availability of backup support, and personal inclinations. Most people feel that parents should be home with a very sick child and that child care is appropriate only for mildly ill children. In a study at a Colorado company, among 17 percent of employees who had lost time from work due to sick children, 65 percent cited not wanting to leave the children home alone as the reason for their absence. While 25 percent did not know anyone to care for their sick child, 22 percent could not afford the cost of this care on top of their regular child care expenses.[17]

FINDING CHILD CARE

The major problem for employed parents and a leading cause of absenteeism is finding care that meets their needs and their children's. The difficulty may be either a lack of information on how and where to find care, or a paucity of care, given particular preferences for location, hours, cost, and quality (see Chapter 2). In one study, 39 percent of parents cited affordability, 16 percent scheduling, and 27 percent transportation as a problem in their search for care.[18]

In other studies, 20 to 50 percent of parents have reported finding the search for child care a struggle. For example, in the *Fortune* study, 20 percent of the parents had a "difficult" or "very difficult" time finding child care. Infant care was especially difficult to find. One third of the parents with infants in the study for *Fortune* reported difficulty, as did 65 percent across three different corporate needs assessment surveys.[19–21] (See Chapter 2.)

This difficulty can lead to a sense of general frustration. One study found that of new working mothers reporting no problems finding and arranging child care, 49 percent were very satisfied with their lives. Of new mothers with serious problems finding care, only 34 percent were very satisfied.[22] Emlen and Koren found that employed mothers with children under twelve who report difficulty finding child care are twice as likely to report worry or stress about child care as those who do make satisfactory arrangements, twice as likely to say that combining work and family responsibilities is difficult, and many times more likely to feel that child care is difficult to continue or maintain.[23] The study for *Fortune* revealed that parents who had problems finding child care were far more likely to be absent than others.[24]

CHILD CARE BREAKDOWNS

Child care breakdowns are likely to occur when parents use multiple sources of care, the care is of poor quality, or there is one caregiver (as in family child care or in-home care as opposed to center care) who may be unable to care for the children due to his or her own illness or family problems.

The backup arrangements parents make determine whether these breakdowns will result in absences.

Employed parents are typically forced to make several child care arrangements per child, and these arrangements can be tenuous.[25] Two studies, one conducted at New York University and another at Merck & Co., found that parents had an average of 1.7 child care arrangements for each child under sixteen.[26, 27] Several studies have found a strong link between the number of child care arrangements that parents use and the number of times these arrangements break down: The more arrangements, the more likely they are to fall apart.[28, 29]

For research on work and family life, parents are commonly asked, "Approximately how many times in the last three months did you have to make special arrangements because your usual child care arrangement fell through because, for example, your child care provider was sick or quit?" In the study for *Fortune*, 40 percent of employed parents had at least one child care breakdown, and about one quarter had between two and five breakdowns during that three-month period. Child care breakdowns also cause stress. The study for *Fortune* found that one third of the parents who experienced child care breakdowns were nervous or stressed frequently, compared to 17 percent of those who had no trouble maintaining their child care arrangements.[30]

The breakdown of child care can even have physical health repercussions. The study for *Fortune* found that the more often parents had to make special child care arrangements, the more likely they were to report stress-related health problems such as shortness of breath, pounding or racing heart, back or neck pains, overeating, drinking more alcohol, smoking more, or taking more tranquilizers.

Parents whose child care arrangements break down are more likely than those without breakdowns to come to work late, leave early, or be absent. In the *Fortune* study, about 39 percent of parents had come to work late or left early in the last three months, with 20 percent doing so three or more times. Of those who missed part of the workday, 72 percent had done so because of family obligations.[31] A survey at Allstate Insurance Company found that almost half (49 percent) of parents had been late or left early at least five times in the past three months due to child care problems.[32] Overall, women miss more time than men.

Stress and Job Performance

A significant proportion of workers report that family concerns reduce their productivity and effectiveness at work. In five company surveys, about one half of the women and more than one third of the men report that child care responsiblities affect their work to some degree.[33]

One factor that affects employed parents' well-being and productivity at work is their satisfaction with their child care arrangements. Stress is also linked to the type of child care used. Forty-six percent of the women and 36 percent of the men using out-of-home care reported child care–related stress. When using self-care or sibling care, 50 percent of the women and 30 percent of the men reported stress.[34]

Turnover

In economic downturns as well as good times, companies are concerned about turnover because they want to recoup training investments and avoid the disruption and cost of replacements. There is growing concern about the scarcity of talent in the marketplace, as well as workplace and societal changes that have diminished company loyalty and made staff retention difficult. Most important, turnover is expensive.

J. Douglas Phillips of Merck & Co., Inc., reviewed several cost-of-turnover studies and found that the loss of an exempt employee costs the company about 1.5 times his or her annual salary. Nonexempt turnover costs are estimated to be about .75 times the annual salary of the particular position. Turnover incurs hidden costs, beyond the processing and relocation costs that companies typically measure. According to Phillips, these visible costs make up less than half the cost of turnover, while hidden costs make up the remainder — including the inefficiency of incoming employees (the average adjustment period for a new employee is estimated to be 12.5 months), coworkers adjusting to incoming employees, and the vacant position awaiting appointment.[35]

While it is widely believed that it is lack of job satisfaction that leads to voluntary employee turnover, the way an employee feels about the company has a greater impact on his or her decision to remain at the company than the job does.[36] In other words, an employee may be dissatisfied with the job but still view the organization positively.

Employees' attitudes toward their companies may improve if employers help to solve their child care problems. Studies of employee and employer *perceptions* after a child care program or child care study is instituted show this to be the case. A 1984 study by Burud, Aschbacher, and McCroskey of 178 employers, most of whom offered on-site centers, found that managers "believed" company child care programs affected turnover, productivity, morale, and re-cruitment positively. A Florida Department of Administra-tion study of Ina S. Thompson Child Care Center users found that 93 percent of the center users would consider child care before changing jobs.

General Evaluations of Employer-Supported Child Care Programs

Very few companies have evaluated their child care initia-tives, and the option they have most thoroughly researched is the on- or near-site center because it is the most tangible option — the easiest for nonparent decision makers to grasp and the easiest for newspapers to photograph.

Sixteen studies on employer-sponsored child care cen-ters are reviewed in Figure 3.1. These studies examine managers' perceptions of the effects of a center, examine perceptions of parents using a center, and provide an ex-perimental comparison of center users and nonusers over a period of time. These studies reveal that there are im-portant differences between how managers and employ-ees perceive on-site child care's effect on productivity and the actual effect it has. Employers and center users are most likely to think that absenteeism and morale have been improved by center usage, while experimental stud-ies indicate that reduced turnover and improved recruit-ment are the greatest benefits. It is to be noted, however, that the centers that were studied did not provide "get well" rooms for mildly ill children as part of the program. Had they done so, absenteeism rates might have been positively affected.

Figure 3.1
STUDIES OF EMPLOYER-SUPPORTED CHILD CARE CENTERS

A. MANAGERS' PERCEPTIONS

Research Site	Researcher/Cite	Sample	Research Design	Major Findings
Multiple Companies — National with Child Care	Perry, 1978[37]	58 employers, most with on-site centers	Survey of manager perceptions	Two thirds or more of managers believed that the child care program helped recruit, lowered absenteeism, and improved attitudes toward company.
Statewide Survey of Employers — Minnesota	AAUW, 1987[38]	563 employers with and without child care	Survey of manager perceptions in 200 randomly selected companies and subsequent interviews	More than two thirds of companies believed that child care support would decrease absenteeism and tardiness and increase productivity, recruitment, retention, and morale.
Multiple Companies — National with Child Care	Magid, 1983[39]	204 employers with child care programs, mostly on-site	Survey of manager perceptions	Asked to rank the five most significant effects of their child care program, managers listed recruitment, morale, lower absenteeism, and turnover.
Multiple Companies — National with Child Care	Burud et al., 1984[40]	178 employers, most with on-site centers	Survey of manager perceptions	Managers believed that turnover, productivity, morale, and recruitment were positively affected by center while absenteeism and tardiness were reduced.
Statewide Survey of Employers — New York	New York State Commission on Child Care, 1987[41]	1,041 employers with and without child care	Survey of manager perceptions	Belief in child care's ability to improve work performance was related to company size, with larger companies more likely to believe that recruitment, retention, absenteeism, tardiness, stress, and morale are positively affected.

B. EMPLOYEES' PERCEPTIONS

Research Site	Researcher/Cite	Sample	Research Design	Major Findings
State of New York Children's Place, Albany, NY	WRI, 1980[42]	88 users of center 1 year after opening	Post-survey of user (66 percent response)	35 percent of users said center enabled them to stay working; 73 percent said absences declined; 47 percent said productivity increased; 83 percent said they worried less.
Methodist Hospital	Burud, 1984[43]	123 users of center	Post-survey of user perceptions (71 percent response)	Center helped keep 41 percent of users; 51 percent said center was a factor in accepting job; 61 percent said productivity improved; 79 percent said morale increased.
Kid's Play, State of Wisconsin Pilot Day Care Center	Wisconsin State Department of Employment Relations, 1987[44]	56 users, 35 supervisors of center users	User perceptions surveyed before enrollment, 5 months after opening, and 17 months after; manager perceptions also surveyed	89 percent of users satisfied with center quality; 73 percent said center helped them be more productive; 82 percent said center reduced worry and had positive effect on scheduling.
Ina S. Thompson Child Care Center — State of Florida	Florida Department of Administration, 1987[45]	37–62 users, 42 supervisors of center users	User perceptions surveyed 9 months after opening and users interviewed 1 year later; interviews with managers	Users reported positive effects on work. Center helped reduce worry about children, 49 percent said they were absent less, 60 percent were late less, and 93 percent would consider child care before changing jobs.
Multiple Companies — National	Dawson et al., 1984[46]	311 employees in 29 companies with various child care programs	Post-test of employees using company-sponsored child care programs	Program users likely to recommend employer, continue with company, work overtime. Child care affected acceptance of promotion. Center yielded greater effects than referrals or financing.

C. EXPERIMENTAL STUDIES COMPARING USERS AND NONUSERS

Research Site	Researcher/Cite	Sample	Research Design	Major Findings
Federal CEO — Washington, D.C.	Krug et al., 1972[47]	50 parents from center, 50 in control group	Pre/post-test users compared to control group	Center users had greater increase in sick leave. Annual leave taken by users decreased after center opened; it decreased more for non-users.
Control Data Consortium — Minneapolis, MN	Milkovich and Gomez, 1976[48]	30 center users, 30 parent nonusers, 30 nonparents	Post-test of center users compared to 2 control groups	Lower employee absenteeism and turnover rates were related to enrollment in the center, while no relationship to job performance was found.
North Carolina, Textile Firm	Youngblood and Chambers-Cook, 1984[49]	410 people in company with center and 3 divisions of another firm with no center	Comparisons of employees in firm with center and those in firm without	Center users higher on job satisfaction, commitment, organizational climate, and lower on turnover. A 19 percent drop in absenteeism and 63 percent drop in turnover rate in company with center.
Catherine McAuley Health Center — Anne Arbor, MI	Marquart, 1988[50]	86 parents using hospital-based child care center or family day care program, matched to group of other child care users	Pre/post-test of hospital center users compared to users of hospital-sponsored family day care and parents using other child care	Users had decreased absences of 1½ days per employee. Recruitment, retention, and recommending employer more likely among users. No differences in job satisfaction, stress, or turnover.
Union Bank — Los Angeles, CA	Ransom and Burud, 1988[51]	87 users 1 year before center and 1 year later	Pre/post-test of users compared to control group, parents on waiting list and other bank employees	Center users absent 1.7 days less than other parents; maternity leaves were 1.2 weeks shorter for center users; 61 percent of job applicants said center was a factor in accepting a job at banks. Turnover and public relations also positively affected.
Dominion Bank — Roanoke, VA	Burge and Stewart, 1988[53]	400 randomly selected employees	Post-survey of all employees and users	Users reported that the center helped reduce absenteeism and aided recruitment and improved productivity.

Source: D. E. Friedman, *Linking Work-Family Issues to the Bottom Line* (New York: The Conference Board, 1991), pp. 41–54.

BENEFITS TO CHILDREN AND SOCIETY

Over the past 20 years, many studies have been conducted to assess the impact of high-quality and more typical early childhood programs on the development and later educational success of children, particularly low-income children. The results have been mixed. In the most extensive and rigorous research, a consortium of researchers conducted follow-up studies of eleven *model* high-quality programs and compared the findings with control groups.[54] The consortium's most significant findings were:

Short-term improvement in intellectual performance. The consortium concluded that early education "produced an increase in low-income children's intelligence test scores that lasted for several years."[55] As the program children grew older, their IQ gains disappeared. Speculation on the causes of this reversal include the lower quality of subsequent schooling, the loss of the comprehensive services that model programs provided (e.g., health and social services), and the long-term effects of poverty.

Short-term improvement in language and mathematical achievement. Of the 18 tests of reading and mathematics achievement, only three were significant. The pooled results of the mathematics tests revealed statistically significant and robust gains for program participants in the third grade. By the sixth grade, however, these gains had dissipated. On reading tests, program children had made mild, statistically significant gains by the third grade, but these disappeared by the fourth grade.[56]

Some evidence of improved school performance.
One of the 11 studies found evidence that quality child care improved the school performance of some students. The ten-year follow-up of the Syracuse Family Development Research Program found that in the seventh and eighth grades, "girls but not boys benefitted from the Syracuse intervention. Multiple sources of data support this conclusion, including school grade average data, school attendance data, and teacher ratings."[57] More specifically, it was found that three fourths of the program girls had C or better average, and none were failing, whereas more than half of the control group girls had C (or worse) averages, and 16 percent were failing. Furthermore, none of the program girls had more than 20 absences, while 31 percent of the control group had more than 20 absences. These findings, however, were not supported at the other study sites.

Less special education. In four of the long-term studies, 13 percent of the program children and 31 percent of the control children had been placed in special education classes.

Increased likelihood of graduating from high school. The Syracuse study found that 53 percent of their fourth and eighth graders who attended preschool expected to remain in high school, as compared to 28 percent of the control group children.[58] The four projects that followed the children through high school found that 65 percent of the program children graduated from high school, as opposed to 52 percent of the control children.[59] This difference was statistically significant. The results were most significant for the High/Scope

Foundation's Ypsilanti Perry Preschool Project, in which 67 percent of the program children completed high school, whereas only 49 percent of the control children did. In addition, 39 percent attended college or job training programs, compared to 21 percent of the controls.[60] The results of the Perry Preschool Project, however, are controversial because the study was conducted under special conditions and its results have never been duplicated. Conducted in the 1960s, the project followed its experimental and control groups to their eighteenth year. Critics of the project cite that it used a very small sample of children, that these children were extremely low-income and had very low IQs (in the 60 to 90 range), and that the program was a highly interventionist one that may not be replicable in inner-city neighborhoods in the 1990s.

Fewer juvenile delinquency offenses. Two studies provided evidence on reduced criminal behavior. The most dramatic documentation of this can be found in the Syracuse intervention. Their program children had a 6 percent rate of juvenile delinquency as opposed to a 22 percent rate for the children in the control group. Also, the program children had only minor offenses, whereas some of the control children had committed burglary, robbery, and physical or sexual assaults. The court and probation costs for the program children were $12,000, where they were $107,000 for the control group.[61] The Perry Preschool Project found that 31 percent of their program children were arrested for criminal acts as against 51 percent of the control group.[62]

Lower teen pregnancy rates. Two of the four long-term studies found lower rates of teen pregnancy. Neither project found preschool to reduce pregnancies by a statistically significant amount. In the Perry Preschool Project, the rate was 68 pregnancies per 100 program women, and 117 pregnancies per 100 women in the control group. The follow-up study found that seven out of eight program girls who became pregnant returned to high school, whereas one in six of the controls did.[63] In reviewing these results, Ron Haskins, Human Resources Minority Council of the Committee on Ways and Means, concluded, "Although not overwhelming, both of these results suggest that quality preschool programs may have moderate impact on the frequency or the consequences of teen pregnancy."[64]

Higher employment rates. Three of the four long-term follow-up studies found no links between preschool attendance and later employment. However, the Perry Preschool Project found that their preschool attendees were more likely to hold jobs (50 percent vs. 32 percent), support themselves by their own or their spouse's earnings (45 percent vs. 25 percent), and be more satisfied with work (42 percent vs. 26 percent).[65]

Less reliance on welfare. Data on whether or not children who have attended model early childhood programs are less reliant on welfare are sparse. The Perry Preschool Project found significant links: at age nineteen years, only 18 percent were on public assistance, as compared to 32 percent of the control group. In addition, the average welfare payment for program children was $633, compared to $1,509 for the control group children.[66] The only other study on this issue, however, found that the proportion of the control group that relied on nongovernment support as their primary income source was higher than the proportion of program participants.

Some evidence that program families have more positive views. The Syracuse intervention found that program families tended to value constructive behavior, education, and the family unit. Program children had more positive feelings about themselves. Lally and his colleagues report that the message arising from interviews with the program families was a proactive approach to life or a belief that one can take steps to reach one's full potential. This stood in contrast to the control families, who tended to emphasize that one should seek to survive or get by.[67] There is less evidence of this finding from the other long-term studies (although perhaps other studies put less emphasis on building family strength), leading Haskins to conclude that the impact on "the attitudes of students and parents is not persuasive."[68]

Overall the results of model child care intervention programs for at-risk children can be summarized as follows:

- There is strong evidence that model preschool programs improve children's IQ for the short term and reduce their placement in special education.

- There is moderate evidence that model preschool programs decrease grade retention and increase the likelihood of graduating from high school.

- The impact of other measures of school and life success is not conclusive.

In reviewing these findings, it is important to remember that they are the results of studying high-quality model programs, rather than more typical child care programs. It is particularly important to remember this in the case of the Ypsilanti Perry Preschool Project.

The Perry Preschool Project: Long-Term Benefits

Despite the controversy over the Perry Preschool Project, it is one of the few comprehensive, longitudinal studies on the effects of early intervention we have that has attempted to generate a cost-benefit analysis. Many claims for early childhood education have been made on the basis of this study, but it is important to keep in mind, as mentioned above, that the program was conducted in the 1960s under special conditions. As a result, we cannot extend its findings beyond the highly disadvantaged sample the study used and generalize them for the larger population. With these cautions in mind, see Figures 3.2 and 3.3. They show the results of the Perry Preschool Project cost-benefit analysis.

The Long-Term Benefits of Head Start

The studies of the 11 programs described above were carried out in model programs under ideal circumstances, including skilled researchers, highly trained caregivers, and generous budgets. But do more typical early childhood programs have a similar effect? The range of quality in our child care system makes this a difficult question to answer. A review of Head Start programs, however, suggests that there can be

77

Figure 3.2
ECONOMIC COSTS AND BENEFITS
TO TAXPAYERS THROUGH AGE NINETEEN

(Estimates are in 1981 dollars discounted at 3 percent)	
Cost of one-year program	**$4,818**
Benefits to taxpayers	
Savings on public school education	5,113
Tax payments on additional earnings of $642	161
Reduced welfare payments	601
Saving in justice system costs	1,233
Subtotal	**7,108**
Net Benefit (Benefits minus Cost)	**$2,290**
A RETURN OF $1.47 PER $1 INVESTED	

Adapted from: J. R. Berrueta-Clement, L. J. Schweinhart, W. S. Barnett, A. S. Epstein, and D. P. Weikart, *Changed Lives: The Effects of the Perry Pre-School Program on Youths Through Age 19* (Ypsilanti, Michigan: High/Scope Press, 1984), p. 91.

benefits from more typical programs as well. Although Head Start is based on a well-tested model with performance standards that combine comprehensive services with education and parental involvement, individual Head Start programs can vary considerably in quality. A 1985 review of 120 different Head Start programs by McKey, Condelli, Ganson, Barrett, McConkey, and Plantz found:

> Children enrolled in Head Start enjoy significant
> immediate gains in the cognitive test scores,
> socio-emotional test scores and health status. In
> the long run, cognitive and socio-emotional test
> scores of former Head Start students do not
> remain superior to those of disadvantaged
> children who did not attend Head Start.
> However, a small subset of studies find that

Figure 3.3
COSTS AND BENEFITS OF CHILD CARE
OVER LIFETIME

(Estimates are in 1981 dollars discounted at 3 percent)	
Cost of one-year program	**$4,818**
Additional costs and benefits for program participants over their lifetime	
Cost to taxpayers	
Secondary education	−704
Benefits to taxpayers	
Taxes paid by program participant	$4,580
Welfare reduction	15,815
Crime reduction	1,871
Previous benefits to taxpayers	7,108
Subtotal	**28,670**
Net Benefit	**$23,852**
A RETURN OF $5.95 PER $1 INVESTED	

Adapted from: J. R. Berrueta-Clement, L. J. Schweinhart, W. S. Barnett, A. S. Epstein, and D. P. Weikart, *Changed Lives: The Effects of the Perry Pre-School Program on Youths Through Age 19* (Ypsilanti, Michigan: High/Scope Press, 1984), p. 91.

former Head Starters are more likely to be promoted to the next grade and are less likely to be assigned to special education classes. Head Start also has aided families by providing health, social, and educational services and by linking families with services available in the community. Finally, educational, economic, health care, social service, and other institutions have been influenced by Head Start staff and parents to provide benefits to both Head Start and non-Head Start families in their respective communities.[69]

A WORD ON THE PUBLIC'S
AMBIVALENCE TOWARD CHILD CARE

Despite some promising signs from the research on the benefits of child care, the public's continuing ambivalence toward nonmaternal care is partly responsible for the slow national response to meeting child care needs. Even today, there is some concern that a mother's outside employment and absence from the home can harm her children. A thorough review of the research, however, reveals that children are not necessarily harmed or helped by their mothers' employment or their care by others. A number of other factors are important, including the attitudes of both mother and family toward employment. If the mother does not believe she should be employed, or if the father is opposed to his wife's employment, then family stress can result and affect the child. Conversely, if the mother and father feel the mother's work is integral to the family's stability or to her own well-being, then the children can prosper.[70] In addition, parents are affected by the conditions of their jobs such as the number of hours they work and how demanding and hectic their jobs are. These conditions can spill over and affect the child.[71]

There has been a substantial amount of work done on how mother-child attachment is affected by a mother's employment. When large numbers of mothers began to join the work force in the 1960s and 1970s, researchers concentrated on the potential harm that could be caused. They examined the child's emotional relationship with the mother because this relationship was considered the cornerstone of a child's subsequent development. Mothers, rather than fathers, were the subjects of these studies. During this same period, the father's lack of employment was examined as potentially harmful for the child.[72]

In reviewing the attachment studies to determine if beyond-the-family child care could shift infants' or young children's primary attachment from their parents to their caregivers, Thomas Gamble and Edward F. Zigler from Yale University found the chance that child care could "prevent the formation of primary attachments to parents, or cause them to be directed elsewhere, seems small indeed."[73] Studies show that young children are capable of becoming attached to many people — their brothers, sisters, caregivers, and grandparents — but their primary attachment is to their mothers and fathers.

In 1987, a group of 16 leading experts, who had previously disagreed strongly about the effects of maternal employment on infants, was convened by the National Center for Clinical Infant Programs and Edward F. Zigler from Yale University to assess what was known from the attachment research. They concluded:

> When parents have choices about selection and utilization of supplementary care for their infants and toddlers and have access to stable child care arrangements featuring skilled, sensitive, and motivated caregivers, there is every reason to believe that both children and families can thrive.[74]

Thus, among the factors that affect children when their mothers and fathers are employed, of particular significance is the quality of the child care itself.

REFERENCES

1. R. M. Steers and S. R. Rhodes, "Major Influences on Employee Attendance: A Process Model," *Journal of Applied Psychology,* Vol. 63, No.4 (1978), pp. 391–407.

2. E. Galinsky, D. E. Friedman, and C. A. Hernandez, *The Corporate Reference Guide to Work-Family Programs* (New York, Families and Work Institute, 1991).

3. E. Galinsky and D. Hughes, "The Fortune Magazine Child Care Study," paper presented at the Annual Convention of the American Psychological Association, New York, August 1987.

4. E. Galinsky, *Child Care and Productivity* (New York: Families and Work Institute, 1988).

5. A. C. Emlen, "Child Care, Work and Family," paper presented at the Annual Convention of the American Psychological Association, New York, August 1987.

6. E. Galinsky, 1988.

7. A. C. Emlen and P. E. Koren, *Hard to Find and Difficult to Manage: The Effects of Child Care on the Workplace* (Portland, OR: Regional Research Institute for Human Services, Portland State University, 1984).

8. M. Shinn, B. Ortiz-Torrez, A. Morris, P. Simko, and N. Wong, "Child Care Patterns, Stress and Job Behaviors among Working Parents," paper presented at the Annual Convention of the American Psychological Association, New York, August 1987.

9. U.S. Bureau of the Census, *Male-Female Differences in Work Experience, Occupation, and Earnings,* Household Economic Studies Series, 10, 70 (Washington, DC: GPO, 1987).

10. *Coors Child Care Needs Assessment: Proposal and Recommendations* (Denver: Coors Company, 1987).

11. A. C. Emlen, P. E. Koren, and D. Louise, *1987 Dependent Care Survey: Sisters of Providence, Final Report* (Portland, OR: Regional Research Institute for Human Services, Portland State University Press, 1987).

12. B. Willer, S. L. Hofferth, E. E. Kisker, P. Divine-Hawkins, E. Farquhar, and F. B. Glanz, *The Demand and Supply of Child Care in 1990* (Washington, DC: National Association for the Education of Young Children; U.S. Department of Health and Human Services, Administration on Children, Youth, and Families; U.S. Department of Education, Office of the Undersecretary, 1991).

13. E. Galinsky and D. Hughes, 1987.

14. J. Fernandez, *Child Care and Corporate Productivity: Resolving Family/Work Conflicts* (Lexington, MA: Lexington Books, D.C. Heath Co., 1986).

15. A. C. Emlen et al., 1987.

16. Regional Research Institute for Human Services, *Employee Profiles: 1987 Dependent Care Survey, Selected Companies* (Portland, OR: Portland State University, 1987).

17. K. Hynes, *Employee Survey for Manville's Dependent Care Task Team* (Denver: unpublished data, 1988).

18. D. E. Friedman, *Linking Work-Family Issues to the Bottom Line* (New York: The Conference Board, 1991).

19. E. Galinsky and D. Hughes, 1987.

20. E. Galinsky, 1988.

21. R. Lurie, E. Galinsky, and D. Hughes, "Resources for Child Care Management," unpublished raw data, Bank Street College, 1987.

22. National Council of Jewish Women, *Accommodating Pregnancy in the Workplace* (New York: NCJW Center for the Child, November 1987).

23. A. C. Emlen and P. Koren, 1984.

24. E. Galinsky and D. Hughes, 1987.

25. S. B. Kamerman, *Parenting in an Unresponsive Society: Managing Work and Family Life* (New York, Free Press, 1980).

26. M. Shinn et al., 1987.

27. E. Galinsky and D. Hughes, "Merck Study," unpublished raw data, Bank Street College, 1985.

28. M. Shinn et al., 1987.

29. E. Galinsky and D. Hughes, 1987.

30. E. Galinsky and D. Hughes, 1987.

31. E. Galinsky and D. Hughes, 1987.

32. T. A. Oleno, *The Allstate Child Care Survey* (Northbrook, IL: Allstate Research and Planning Center, 1988).

33. D. E. Friedman, 1991.

34. A. C. Emlen and P. Koren, 1984.

35. J. D. Phillips, *Employee Turnover and the Bottom Line* (Rahway, NJ: Merck & Co., Inc., 1989).

36. L. R. Watts and H. C. White, "Assessing Employee Turnover," *Personnel Administration* (April 1988), p. 81.

37. K. Perry, *Employers and Day Care: Establishing Services Through the Work Force* (Washington, DC: U.S. Department of Labor, Women's Bureau, GPO, 1978).

38. American Association of University Women, *Employer-Supported Child Care in Michigan* (Lansing, MI: AAUW, 1987).

39. R. Y. Magid, *Child Care Initiatives for Working Parents* (New York: American Management Association, 1983).

83

40. S. L. Burud, P. R. Aschbacher, and J. McCroskey, *Employer-Supported Child Care: Investing in Human Resources* (Boston: Auburn House Publishing Company, 1984).

41. New York State Commission on Child Care, *Employers and Child Care in New York State* (Albany: 1987).

42. WRI, *Children's Place at the Plaza, Evaluation Report* (Albany: WRI, 1980).

43. S. L. Burud, *Productivity Impact Study of Kathy Kredel Nursery School* (Arcadia, California: Methodist Hospital of Southern California, 1984).

44. Wisconsin Department of Employment Relations, *State of Wisconsin Pilot Day Care Center Final Report* (Madison: 1987).

45. Florida Department of Administration, *Florida Child Care Pilot Project,* Final Report to the Florida Legislature (Tallahassee: 1987).

46. A. G. Dawson, C. S. Mikel, C. S. Lorenz, and J. King, *An Experimental Study of the Effects of Employer-Sponsored Child Care Services in Selected Employee Behaviors* (Chicago: Foundation for Human Services, Inc., 1984).

47. D. N. Krug, V. E. Palmour, and M. C. Ballassai, Office of Economic Opportunity Child Development Center (Rockville, Maryland: Westat, Inc., 1972).

48. G. T. Milkovich and L. R. Gomez, "Day Care and Selected Work Behaviors," *Academy of Management Journal,* Vol. 19, No. 1 (1976), pp. 111–115.

49. S. A. Youngblood and K. Chambers-Cook, "Child Care Assistance Can Improve Employee Attitudes and Behavior," *Personnel Administrator* (February 1984), pp. 45–95.

50. J. M. Marquart, "A Pattern Matching Approach to Link Program Theory and Evaluation Data: The Case of Employer-Sponsored Child Care," Ph.D. Dissertation, Cornell University, 1988.

51. C. Ransom and S. L. Burud, *Productivity Impact Study,* unpublished report (Pasadena: Union Bank Child Care Center, 1988).

52. C. Ransom, P. Aschbacher, and S. L. Burud, *The Return of an Investment in Child Care Benefits — Is It Real? The Union Bank Story,* unpublished manuscript (Pasadena: 1988).

53. D. L. Burge and D. L. Stewart, *The Dominion Bank Story* (Roanoke: Virginia Tech. University, 1988).

54. I. Lazar and R. Darlington, "Lasting Effects of Early Education: A Report of the Consortium for Longitudinal Studies," *Monographs of the Society for Research in Child Development,* Vol. 47(2–3), No. 195, (1982).

55. I. Lazar and R. Darlington, 1982, p. 48.

56. I. Lazar and R. Darlington, 1982.

57. J. R. Lally, P. Mangione, A. Honig, and D. Wittner, "More Pride, Less Delinquency: Findings from the Ten-Year Follow-up Study of the Syracuse University Family Development Research Program," *Zero to Three* (April 1988), pp. 13–17.

58. J. R. Lally et al., 1988.

59. R. Haskins, "Beyond Metaphor: The Efficacy of Early Childhood Education," *American Psychologist*, Vol. 44, No. 2 (February 1989), pp. 274–282.

60. D. P. Weikart, Testimony at the U.S. Congressional Subcommittee on Education and Health, Joint Economic Committee, February 26, 1990, p. 4.

61. J. R. Lally et al., 1988.

62. D. P. Weikart, 1990.

63. D. P. Weikart, 1990.

64. R. Haskins, 1989, p. 276.

65. D. P. Weikart, 1990.

66. D. P. Weikart, 1990.

67. J. R. Lally et al., 1988.

68. R. Haskins, 1989, p. 276.

69. R. H. McKey, L. Condelli, H. Ganson, B. Barrett, C. McConkey, and M. Plantz, *The Impact of Head Start on Children, Families and Communities* (Washington, DC: CSR, Inc., 1985), p. 1.

70. A. E. Gottfried, A. W. Gottfried, and K. Bathurst, "Maternal Employment, Family Environment, and Children's Development: Infancy through the School Years," in *Maternal Employment and Children's Development: Longitudinal Research*, A. E. Gottfried and A. W. Gottfried, eds. (Los Angeles: 1988), pp. 11–56.

71. C. Howes, M. Shinn, L. M. Sakai, D. Phillips, E. Galinsky, and M. Whitebook, *Race, Social Class, and Maternal Working Conditions as Influences on Children's Development in Child Care* (Los Angeles: UCLA, in preparation).

72. U. Bronfenbrenner and A. Crouter, "Work and Family through Time and Space," in S. B. Kamerman and S. C. Hayes, eds., *Families That Work: Children in a Changing World* (Washington, DC: National Academy Press, 1982), pp. 39–83.

73. T. J. Gamble and E. Zigler, "Effects of Infant Day Care: Another Look at the Evidence," *American Journal of Orthopsychiatry*, Vol. 56, No. 1 (January 1986), p. 29.

74. National Center for Clinical Infant Programs, press release, November 25, 1987, Washington, DC.

CHAPTER 4

The Cost of Typical and High-Quality Child Care

The National Child Care Survey 1990 provides the most recent data on the per hour costs that families with children under five spend for child care. It reveals that 56 percent of these families pay for child care, while 68 percent of families with full-time employed mothers do so. The expenditures for employed mothers range from $1.11 per hour for relative care to $2.30 per hour for in-home, nonrelative care.[1] For nonemployed mothers, the costs range from $1.89 per hour for center care to $2.20 for family child care.

The average yearly price that families with employed mothers paid for all types of care for preschool children — not just center-based programs — was $3,150, not including subsidies. For families with employed mothers, center-based care was $3,173 a year; family child care was $2,565; relative care was $2,054; and in-home care was $3,565. (These annual figures reflect the number of cost per hour, multiplied by the number of hours per day and weeks per year the arrangement is typically used.)

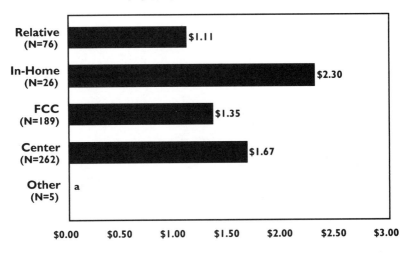

Figure 4.1A
MEAN HOURLY EXPENDITURE FOR YOUNGEST UNDER FIVE BY TYPE OF PRIMARY ARRANGEMENT, EMPLOYED MOTHERS PAYING FOR CARE ONLY

[a] Fewer than 10 cases.

Source: Families and Work Institute, 1993.

The National Association for the Education of Young Children (NAEYC) estimates that the cost of good-quality center-based care should range from $6,364 to $8,345.[2] However, others have contended that the price should be much higher, closer to $12,000.[3] The differential between the 1990 cost figures and the higher-quality estimates largely reflects the low salaries paid to child care program staff—the chief cause of high turnover, which, in turn, contributes to poor quality. In any case, a substantial number of families with children under the age of five cannot afford to pay the $6,364 to $8,345 figure for good quality.

Figure 4.1B

MEAN HOURLY EXPENDITURE FOR YOUNGEST UNDER FIVE BY TYPE OF PRIMARY ARRANGEMENT, NONEMPLOYED MOTHERS PAYING FOR CARE ONLY

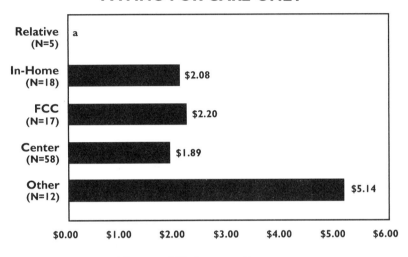

Type of Primary Arrangement

[a]Fewer than 10 cases.

Source: S. L. Hofferth, A. Brayfield, S. Deitch, and P. Holcomb, *The National Child Care Survey, 1990* (Washington, DC: The Urban Institute, 1991), pp. 139–144.

At the same time, there are costs to *not* providing high-quality child care. As previously discussed, there may be developmental consequences for children who do not receive individualized attention, who are bored, who are pressured to learn in inappropriate ways, or who are in unsafe settings. There also can be costs for employers when parents depend on unreliable or poor-quality care for their children.

Because both the cost of quality care and the cost of not providing it may be high, there are choices ahead for policy makers and business as the public debates how to provide more quality, how to pay for it, and particularly, whether the need for quality is great enough to warrant public intervention so that everyone might have access to it. This chapter cannot begin to resolve these issues. It does, however, provide some background information on cost that is central to the debate.

This chapter first discusses the trends in the cost of child care over the last quarter of a century, as well as parent fees and the current costs of running typical programs; it then attempts to estimate how much quality costs. Our estimate is a very rough one, and before more exact estimates are calculated, additional research is necessary. Now, we know the fees that programs charge, and we know what parents pay. We can only estimate what programs would have to charge if they met quality standards and paid their staff respectable wages and benefits. We do not know how much of this increased cost parents would be able to afford and how much subsidization from public and private sources would be necessary. We do not have enough data on family child care providers, particularly nonregulated ones. We do not have estimates on the costs of building the necessary infrastructure. Finally, because of the diversity of child care arrangements, we are forced to make some assumptions on price and supply. These gaps in knowledge underscore the need to recruit skilled economists and demographers into child care research.

WHAT DO PARENTS PAY NOW?

As mentioned above, the average yearly 1990 price for all forms of care for preschool children with employed mothers is $3,150. The actual price of care varies regionally, by family income and size, by the age of the youngest child, and by the type of care (see Figure 4.2).

There are several factors to keep in mind regarding parents' fees:

Despite inflation, the cost of child care has remained virtually constant over the last 25 years. Studies have shown that during the 1980s, the fees parents typically paid for child care ranged between $2,000 and $3,000 per year.[4-6] In examining cost data from 1975 and comparing them to figures from 1985, Hofferth and her colleagues found only a very slight increase per hour in all types of care, with the biggest increases in relative and in-home care. In comparing 1975 and 1990, the per hour cost of center care increased by 27 cents and for family child care by 6 cents.[7] (See Figure 4.3.)

Employed mothers with preschool children (children under five) currently spend about 10 percent of their weekly family income on child care. This figure has remained much the same since 1985.

Low-income families spend a greater portion of their incomes on child care than do wealthier families. While low-income families (under $15,000) spend 23 percent of their family income on child care, higher-income families (over $50,000) spend 6 percent.[8] (See Figure 4.4.)

Whether parents pay for their child care largely depends on whether the mother is employed outside the home. Most previous analyses of child care

Figure 4.2

AVERAGE HOURLY EXPENDITURE FOR YOUNGEST CHILD UNDER FIVE
FAMILIES WITH AN EMPLOYED MOTHER
(THOSE PAYING FOR CARE ONLY)

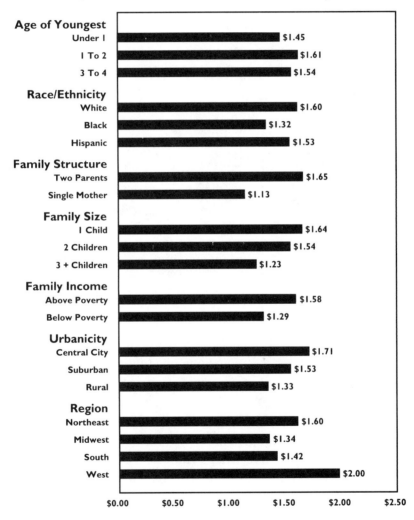

Source: S. L. Hofferth, A. Brayfield, S. Deitch, and P. Holcomb, *The National Child Care Survey, 1990* (Washington, DC: The Urban Institute, 1991), pp. 136–137.

91

Figure 4.3

MEAN HOURLY EXPENDITURE FOR YOUNGEST UNDER FIVE, EMPLOYED MOTHERS PAYING FOR CHILD CARE 1975–1990

(Constant 1990 Dollars)

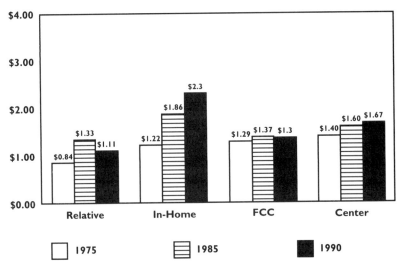

Source: S. L. Hofferth, A. Brayfield, S. Deitch, and P. Holcomb, *The National Child Care Survey, 1990* (Washington, DC: The Urban Institute, 1991), p. 139.

costs have excluded mothers who stay home with their children, despite the fact that many of them want an enriching early education experience for their children. According to The Urban Institute's 1990 National Child Care Survey, in 33 percent of families with the youngest child under age five where the mother is not working outside the home, the child is in some form of nonparental care. Among families with employed mothers whose youngest child is under five years old, as previously stated, 56 percent pay for the care they use. Among

Figure 4.4

MEAN PERCENTAGE OF FAMILY INCOME SPENT ON CHILD CARE BY RACE/ETHNICITY AND FAMILY INCOME, EMPLOYED MOTHERS WITH YOUNGEST CHILD UNDER FIVE PAYING FOR CARE ONLY

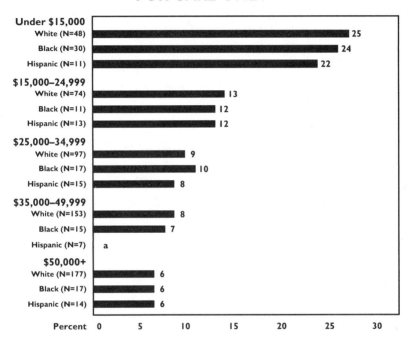

[a] Fewer than 10 cases.

Source: S. L. Hofferth, A. Brayfield, S. Deitch, and P. Holcomb, *The National Child Care Survey, 1990* (Washington, DC: The Urban Institute, 1991), p. 177.

comparable nonemployed mothers, 14 percent pay for their preschoolers' child care arrangements.[9]

Parents almost always make payments for formal child care, occasionally for relative care, and almost never for parent care. For care of preschoolers

93

whose mothers are employed, 90 percent pay for a center, 95 percent pay when family child care is used, 93 percent pay for in-home care, and 39 percent pay relatives. Among families with nonemployed mothers, 12 percent pay their relatives, 83 percent pay their in-home child care, 57 percent pay family child care providers, and 94 percent pay for a child care center. In both types of families, when one or the other parent is the primary child care provider (even when working or when working split shifts), he or she is almost never paid (see Figure 4.5).

The amount parents pay differs by the employment status of the mother and the amount of care used. On average, the National Child Care Survey found that families with employed mothers pay a lower hourly fee for their child care than those with nonemployed mothers, but they use more hours of care each week (37 hours vs. 13 hours). This brings the total weekly expenditure on child care for employed mothers of preschoolers to $63, compared to the $35 per week paid by nonemployed mothers.

ESTIMATING THE FULL COST OF QUALITY
Center-Based Care

What are the costs of running a child care center today? There are several useful budget estimates. The National Child Care Staffing Study provides detailed information on 227 full-day child care centers in five metropolitan areas: Atlanta, Boston, Detroit, Phoenix, and Seattle. Although the sites may not be nationally representative, they do rep-

Figure 4.5

PERCENTAGE PAYING CASH FOR PRIMARY ARRANGEMENT FOR YOUNGEST CHILD UNDER FIVE BY TYPE AND MATERNAL EMPLOYMENT STATUS

Employed Mothers

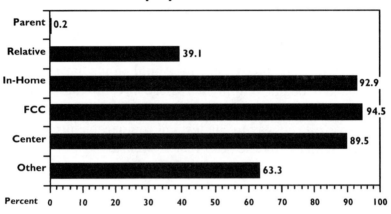

Non-Employed Mothers

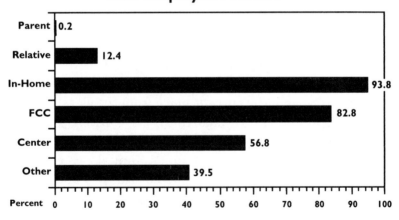

Source: S. L. Hofferth, A. Brayfield, S. Deitch, and P. Holcomb, *The National Child Care Survey, 1990* (Washington, DC: The Urban Institute, 1991), p. 123.

resent the diversity in the child care marketplace and a range of budgets for typical programs. In addition, a Government Accounting Office (GAO) study provides data on the budgets of 265 high-quality programs that have been accredited by the National Academy of Early Childhood Programs, a division of NAEYC. This study found that even these accredited programs paid low salaries to staff, which resulted in high levels of staff turnover.

Using the GAO study as a base, Barbara Willer of NAEYC estimated what the cost of care would be if salaries rose to levels that begin to approach those of comparable professions, a level she calls the "improved estimate," and if salaries rose all the way to the level of comparable professions, which Willer calls the "full-cost estimate."[10]

Both of the new estimates include the use of master teachers and a career ladder for providers, both of which are assumed to reduce turnover and recruit staff. In this model, there are prescribed steps for the career development of providers, with several different levels of expertise for providers to attain. Leading the field would be master teachers and center directors with three years of experience and a master's degree. Salary increases for providers would be based on the educational background of the provider, her or his years of experience, and a comparison with skills required in other jobs, and advancement options would be expanded beyond the current move from the classroom into administration. NAEYC currently is working toward a model of professional development for providers.

As Figure 4.6 indicates, Willer's annual per child cost of center-based care with "improved" salaries and benefits would be $6,364. The "full-cost estimate" raises the price to $8,345.

Figure 4.6
A COMPARISON OF COST ESTIMATES

Estimates based on NCCSS data	Estimates based on GAO study of accredited centers	Improved Estimates (GAO figures plus improved salaries and 10 percent increase in nonpersonnel)	Full Cost Estimates (Improved plus salary increases to comparability and 10 percent increase in nonpersonnel)
Total Groups = 5 Ages = All	Total Groups = 5 Ages = All	Total Groups = 5 Ages = All	Total Groups = 5 Ages = All
Teaching Staff 1 Director @ $20,488 5 Teachers @ $9,975 10 Assistants @ $8,173	Teaching Staff 1 Director @ $24,300 5 Teachers @ $14,100 10 Assistants @ $10,200	Teaching Staff 1 Director @ $30,000 2 Master Teachers @ $22,000 3 Teachers @ $20,000 2.5 Assistant Teachers @ $16,000 2.5 Teaching Assistants @ $13,500	Teaching Staff 1 Director @ $40,000 2 Master Teachers @ $33,000 3 Teachers @ $29,000 2.5 Assistant Teachers @ $23,000 2.5 Teaching Assistants @ $17,500
Total Educational Salaries = $152,088	Total Educational Salaries = $196,800	Total Educational Salaries = $281,000	Total Educational Salaries = $398,000
Total Budget = $241,084	Total Budget = $409,148	Total Budget = $537,928	Total Budget = $711,112
Annual Cost per Child = $2,870	Annual Cost per Child = $4,871	Annual Cost per Child = $6,364	Annual Cost per Child = $8,345

Note: All estimates are based on a program serving 84 children. NCCSS teaching salaries are based on a 35-hour work week for 50 weeks per year, as reported by the NCCSS. The remaining columns calculate salaries for a 40-hour work week, 52 weeks per year. The total budget for Column 1 is the NCCSS average reported center budget. In the other columns, total budget is calculated based on the percentages reported in the GAO study. In Column 2, teaching personnel costs are 74 percent of the total personnel budget, which is 65 percent of the total budget. In Columns 3 and 4, nonpersonnel costs begin with the nonpersonnel costs reported by GAO for accredited centers and adds a 10 percent increase at both steps.

Source: B. Willer, "Estimating the Full Cost of Quality" in B. Willer, ed., *Reaching the Full Cost of Quality in Early Childhood Programs* (Washington, DC: National Association for the Education of Young Children, 1990), p. 61.

Family Child Care

There is very little research on the income and expenses of family child care homes in the United States. The Families and Work Institute bases its estimates of operating budgets on a Family Child Care Budget spread sheet, developed by Kathy Modigliani of Wheelock College, and on business deductions estimated by Tom Copeland for Resources for Child Caring in St. Paul, Minnesota. To include economic and geographic diversity in its estimate, the Families and Work Institute obtained full budgets from providers in the Midwest, Southeast, and West, from providers in rural and urban areas, and from regulated and nonregulated providers. Input from leaders in the family child care field was solicited as well. The sample, however, is in no way representative, and much further work is needed in this area.

Unlike the case of center care, estimating the full cost of quality by projecting improved salaries for providers is more uncertain in the case of family child care. This is mostly because we do not know that salaries actually significantly affect turnover in family child care home situations. Family child care providers may have less attachment to the work force, live closer to their work, and deny nonpecuniary benefits.[11] As a result, the usual work force considerations of salary and benefits may not affect turnover in family child care homes as directly as they do in other fields.

This is not to say that the quality of family child care would not improve even if providers received an infusion of cash. Family care providers do need funds to upgrade facilities in their homes, pursue education on child care, or any number of things to improve the quality of care. It is simply saying that it is unknown whether salary, benefits,

98

and working conditions affect turnover in the family child care field in the way they do other fields.

Family child care providers clearly receive extremely low wages. As Figure 4.7 indicates, according to the 1990 National Child Care Survey, the average family child care provider serves four children in his or her home for 37 hours a week, for 50 weeks, with fees averaging $1.35 an hour per child. This gives an average yearly gross income of $9,990, which yields on average less than $2,500 net over expenses. All expenses for providing care to the children are deductible, including portions of the home and other equipment. All told, the deductible expenses equal $6,481, yielding a taxable income of $3,509. This amount is reduced by $1,021 in federal income taxes and Social Security taxes, so that the net earnings of a family child care provider average $2,488.

In analyzing providers' budgets, Copeland has demonstrated that a nonregulated provider pays more in taxes because she or he is unable to claim expenses associated with the house. Applying Copeland's formula to the typical provider demonstrates that her or his income would increase by $2,700 per year ($1,913 net) by taking advantage of the Child Care Food Program.

The typical provider has one year of college, so comparing her current wages with what she might have earned in another position in the labor force gives an estimate of the true value of quality family child care. Current population reports indicate that such a woman in the civilian labor force in 1987 earns $15,806 on average.[12]

If benefits at 33 percent of salary (national average) are added, it would bring total compensation to $18,150, although the provider still has to pay expenses.[13] This would

Figure 4.7
FAMILY CHILD CARE HOME: ANNUAL BUDGET

	Regulated	Regulated and on CCFP	Nonregulated
Income			
$1.35 hour × 37 hours × 4 children[a]	$9,990	$9,990	$9,990
Child Care Food Program (CCFP)[b]		2,700	
TOTAL INCOME	9,990	12,690	9,990
Deductible Expenses			
House depreciation[c]	380	380	*
Personal property depreciation[d]	142	142	142
Mortgage interest[e]	750	750	*
Property taxes[f]	150	150	*
Utilities[g]	175	175	*
Homeowners insurance[h]	75	75	*
Food[i]	2,550	2,550	2,550
Maintenance and repairs	275	275	275
Toys and materials	600	600	600
Office supplies	200	200	200
Household supplies	200	200	200
Equipment for children	300	300	300
Accountant, bank fees	156	156	156
Transportation	342	342	342
Telephone	80	80	80
Postage	28	28	28
Copying	42	42	42
Advertising	48	48	48
Business entertaining (gifts to children and parents)	258	258	258
Cleaning	102	102	102
Substitute help	158	158	158
Professional dues/meetings/training	170	170	170
	$6,481	$6,481	4,951
Taxable income	3,509	6,209	5,039
Federal income tax[j]	−526	−931	−756
Social Security tax[k]	−496	−877	−712
	−1,021	−1,808	−1,468
Gross Profit	2,488	4,401	3,571
	−0	−0	−1,530
Net Profit	$2,488	4,401	2,041

[a] S. L. Hofferth et al., 1991.
[b] Tom Copeland, 1990.
[c] House depreciation: ($50,000 home × 25 percent T/S × 3.042 percent) (1st year of 7 years).
[d] Appliances, furniture, equipment: $4,000 × 25 percent T/S × 4.29 percent) (1st year of 7 years).
[e] $3,000 × 25 percent T/S.
[f] $600 × 25 percent T/S.
[g] $700 × 25 percent T/S.
[h] $300 × 25 percent T/S.

[i] Food: $.76 for breakfast per child per day; $.41 snack; $1.38 lunch or dinner = $2.55 × 4 children × 5 days × 50 weeks = $2,550; data from the Children's Foundation.
[j] Federal taxes will be 15%, assuming joint family income is below $32,450 for 1990.
[k] Social Security tax: 15.3 percent on 92.35 percent of taxable income. New tax laws allow providers to deduct one half of the amount of their Social Security tax from their income. This calculation is not included.

Source: Families and Work Institute, adapted from Tom Copeland, *The Tax Benefits of Becoming a Regulated Family Child Care Provider* (St. Paul: Resources for Child Caring, 1992).

increase the hourly rate per child (assuming 4 children in care) to $2.45, representing a 81 percent increase over what parents currently pay.

THE SIZE OF THE CHILD CARE INDUSTRY

Using data from the National Child Care Survey, total yearly payments by families with employed and nonemployed mothers to child care programs *outside the child's home* (centers and family child care homes only) can be calculated to equal $11.5 billion. Total yearly fees to all types of settings total $13.6 billion. (See Figure 4.8.)

These figures are similar to an estimate generated by Martin O'Connell of the Bureau of Labor Statistics, who simply multiplied the average weekly fee of $49 (in 1987) by the 6.2 million mothers who reported payments. His estimate of the total yearly cash outlays by parents for child care was $15.5 billion.[14]

Quality improvements, according to our calculations using the National Child Care Survey estimates, would increase the cost of child care services to $21.5 billion (in terms of cash outlays, not including the costs of relative or in-home care). The difference between what parents pay and what quality costs—the "quality gap"—is $10 billion. The federal government contributed approximately $7.7 billion to the child care field in 1991 (including funding from the new child care legislation), with tax credits offsetting $3.9 billion of the $13.6 billion that parents pay. Employer contributions to the field and internal company policies and programs add more than $100 million.

The child care industry has to meet other costs that

Figure 4.8

WHAT PARENTS SPEND ON CHILD CARE

	Mother Employed (7.4 m mothers with youngest child < 5)		Mother Not Employed (6.3 m mothers with youngest child < 5)	
Those Who Use:	**Percent**	**Number**	**Percent**	**Number**
Centers	28	2,072,000	20	1,260,000
Family child care	20	1,480,000	12	756,000
Relatives	19	1,406,000	16	1,008,000
In-home	3	222,000	3	189,000
Parents	28	2,072,000	45	2,835,000
Those Who Pay Cash:	**Percent**	**Number**	**Percent**	**Number**
Centers	90	1,864,800	94	1,184,400
Family child care	95	1,406,000	57	430,920
Relatives	39	548,340	12	120,960
In-home	93	206,460	83	156,870
What They Pay:				
Centers	$1.67 × 38 hours = $63.46/week = $3173/year		$1.89 × 12 hours = $22.68/week = $1134/year	
Family child care	$1.35 × 38 hours = $51.30/week = $2565/year		$2.20 × 14 hours = $30.80/week = $1540/year	
Relatives	$1.11 × 37 hours = $41.07/week = $2054/year		[a]	
In-home	$2.30 × 31 hours = $71.30/week = $3565/year		$2.08 × 13 hours = $27.04/week = $1352/year	
Total Payments:				
Centers	$5,917,010,400		$1,343,109,600	
Family child care	$3,606,390,000		$663,616,800	
Relatives	$1,126,290,360		[a]	
In-home	$736,029,900		$212,088,240	
	$11,385,720,660		**$ 2,218,814,640**	
All Fees: **Centers and Family Child Care** (Only)			**$13,604,535,300** **$11,530,126,800**	

Full Cost of Quality (Centers and Family Child Care)[b]				
Employed Mothers				
Centers	$6364/year	($3.35/hour)	=	$11,867,587,000
Family Child Care	$4655/year	($2.45/hour)	=	$6,544,930,000
Nonemployed Mothers				
Centers	$2010/year	($3.35/hour)	=	2,380,644,000
Family Child Care	$1715/year	($2.45/hour)	=	739,027,800
				$21,532,188,800
		Less Parent Fees		− 11,530,126,800
		Quality Gap		**$10,002,062,000**

[a] Sample size too small to provide accurate amount.

[b] See Figure 4.6 for the NAEYC estimate of quality child care centers. The estimates for the cost of quality family child care are described on pages 98–100.

Source: Families and Work Institute. Based on data from S. L. Hofferth, A. Brayfield, S. Deitch, and P. Holcomb, *The 1990 National Child Care Survey* (Washington, DC: The Urban Institute, 1991).

cannot be passed on to families, which are related to administration, trade associations, publishing, research and advocacy, resource, and referral, as well as capital costs and the cost of regulation. Including these costs brings the estimate of the current industry size up to $18 billion from the $13.6 billion mentioned above. Some of these factors are discussed below.

Start-Up Costs

Capital and start-up costs are rarely passed along to parents. New initiatives by state agencies and employers (banks in particular) can subsidize capital costs associated with supply building. New York State, for instance, has $8 million set aside for the purposes of helping local communities build new centers or renovate existing ones. There is also untapped potential in the Community Reinvestment Act that encourages banks to invest in low-income neighborhoods. Although they are loans, these monies can make a significant difference in local efforts to raise start-up dollars.

A new dimension of corporate involvement in child care is the creation of "funds" or foundation funded projects targeted to communities where participating companies have employees. IBM, AT&T, NYNEX, American Express, Mervyn's, and Target Stores alone have committed about $45 million to supply and quality improvements in child care. Millions more have been contributed by the 137 firms participating in the American Business Collaboration.

Referral Services

Resource and referral agencies, a critical part of the child care system, typically have budgets of less than $500,000. The estimated 300 referral agencies currently in existence, with an average budget of $250,000, operate on about $75 million. About half of the referral agencies depend on government resources for more than 70 percent of their budgets. Almost one third (29 percent) receive 90 to 100 percent of their funding from government. Those with employer contracts tend to rely on these contracts for less than 20 percent of their budgets. About one third of referral agencies charge user fees to the parents who call. These fees generally comprise less than 10 percent of overall budgets.[15]

Training

There is a vast network of agencies, colleges, and universities offering training to child care providers. Some training is offered through government efforts, such as the Job Training Partnership Act (JTPA) and support for the Child Development Associate (CDA) credential, but the overwhelming majority of costs associated with improving caregiver skills are assumed by the caregivers themselves.

The cost of trainers, materials, and other meeting expenses have never been estimated. By including CDA, JTPA, and training offered by referral agencies and child care networks and associations, professional conferences, and seminars, as well as some formal training within the university system, a rough estimate for the nation's child care training costs might be $50 million. The Children's Defense Fund estimates that about $8 million of state government funds are used for training purposes, as are $1.2 million of federal funds.[16]

Regulation

To ensure that programs meet minimal health and safety standards, states assume a monitoring function that is labor intensive and costly. All 50 states have some regulations that must be monitored and enforced. Some cover only child care centers, others have systems of registration for family child care providers, and still others have family child care licensing (see Chapter 2). Several states elicit the help of referral agencies in monitoring compliance with state standards. At an average cost of approximately $10 million per state, the estimated cost of regulation nationally is $500 million.[17]

WHAT HAPPENS TO THE SYSTEM WHEN TYPICAL PROGRAMS RAISE QUALITY INDICATORS

We know that increasing salaries of caregivers and improving staff-child ratios in child care centers raise the likelihood that a high-quality caregiver-child relationship will take place. What then happens to price and accessibility? A few experiments in this area have examined this issue.

Effects of Improving Salaries

Experiments in raising wages in child care centers have occurred in Massachusetts and New York, both of which have launched further state efforts to improve the quality of child care by decreasing turnover among staff. Massachusetts' experience showed that unless a systemic approach is taken, one sector may benefit from the increases while another may not. The state raised the rate of reimbursement for state-funded children. Over a three-year period from 1986 to 1988, $15.2 million was allocated to this effort. Although salaries were raised in subsidized programs and turnover decreased, fee-paying parents in these programs were faced with higher rates. As Fried and Whitebook state in their analysis of the Massachusetts experience, "Without addressing affordability, the issue of inadequate wages simply cannot be resolved."[18] A scholarship fund was then developed to help families whose incomes fell just above the threshold for state subsidization.

New York State initially took a different approach to increasing salaries, partly to avoid the kind of problems that Massachusetts faced. The state's one-time $12 million designation for salary enhancement went to programs, rather than into reimbursement rates. In this way, the program could allocate the funds directly to staff. An initial study of the impact of this program by Marx, Zinsser, and Porter indicated that staff retention was indeed improved. The $12 million reached 10,270 staff, each of whom received an average of $1,200. Before the legislation was enacted, teachers and supervisory staff in New York City had a turnover rate of 42 percent. The following year, this rate had dropped to 22 percent. Other staff vacancies were cut by half as well.[19]

Effects of Improving Ratios

How are cost and quantity of care affected when programs improve their staff-children ratios? In a 1990 Children's Defense Fund report, Gina Adams states:

> To ensure a child's safety and to promote
> emotional and intellectual development, child
> development experts recommend that a single
> caregiver care for no more than three or four
> infants. However, 19 states allow child care
> centers to operate with five or more infants per
> adult, and 13 states allow a single family day

care provider to care for five or more infants and toddlers . . . on the other hand, 20 states met recommended levels for most or all of the six selected age ranges. Experts agree that children's development is hindered when they are cared for in large groups. Yet nearly half (22) of the states have no group size limits whatsoever.[20]

In the past five years, Arizona and Ohio have improved their staff-child ratio requirements, providing an opportunity to examine the ways these changes affect the quality, cost, and availability of child care. In both of these states, there was understandable resistance to the change in the for-profit child care sector and among many parents. It was feared that the improvements would force centers to raise their prices, making child care unaffordable to parents. There was also concern that higher ratios would reduce supply by causing programs to close or to cease offering the more expensive infant care.

In Arizona, it was decided that a gradual phase-in of the new standards might ease some of the negative effects (see Figure 4.9). It became clear that neither programs nor parents suffered the hardships expected. For example, some large child care chains set up operations in Arizona after the new laws took effect, noting that since their chains were committed to high quality, more stringent regulations would enable them to compete more fairly. In addition, the number of centers has increased steadily each year. In 1986, there were 777 centers. By 1990, the number had risen to 1,081. Unfortunately, however, there was no monitoring of the impact on infant care, making it impossible to detect whether there was an increase or decrease in programs serving the youngest children. Furthermore, no data were

Figure 4.9
ARIZONA'S PHASED-IN STANDARDS

Child's Age	Previous Ratios	New Ratios	Effective Date
Under Two	1:8	1:5 or 2:11	7/1/88
Twos	1:10	1:8	7/1/88
Threes	1:15	1:13	7/1/89
Fours	1:20	1:15	7/1/89
Fives	1:25	1:20	1/1/90
School-Age	1:25	1:20	1/1/90

kept on program management, so there is no information on whether salaries were lowered or fees raised. Despite this lack of information, several state officials and child care advocates interviewed for this report stated that the regulations did not seem to hamper the child care market; instead, it was flourishing.

Ohio's experience was similar. In 1985, the state reduced its required ratio for infants from 1:8 to 1:5 or 1:6. Since then, the space for infants in programs has increased by 35 to 50 percent. Despite stricter ratios for other ages, too, there are 30 percent more children in child care. These increases have not occurred because there were more children from a population influx into the state, but because more preschoolers' mothers worked outside the home. As in Arizona, improved standards did not seem to have a negative effect on the child care industry. Further investigations will be necessary to determine the impact on cost and quality.

HARD CHOICES

Despite the above examples of positive results, improving quality in child care, as in other industries, usually reduces affordability: the crux of the public policy problem. We know how to provide quality care, but the vast majority of parents cannot afford it.

Based on the GAO and NAEYC research as well as the Families and Work Institute's estimates for quality care, parents are paying slightly more than half of what true quality costs. (See Figure 4.8 where parent fees total $11.5 million and the full cost of quality care is estimated at $21.5 million.) In an analysis by Suzanne Helburn, John Morris, and Mary Culkin of the University of Colorado at Denver, parents were found to pay approximately 31 percent of the full production costs of a nonprofit center, 55 percent of the full production costs of a for-profit center, and 33 percent of the full costs of a family child care home. These full production costs are based on estimates of the opportunity forgone by child care providers of working in another occupation in which they could earn a higher salary. Helburn and her colleagues concluded that an increase in wages to equal the average amount earned by someone in another field of the same sex, age, and educational level "would increase monthly costs by $263 in a nonprofit center and $121 in a for-profit child care center. For family child care homes, costs would increase on average by $227."[21]

Economists have explained the reasons for considering the implications of funding quality child care:

1. According to Helburn, Morris, and Culkin, child care is a social good:

    Quality care and education is a social good, benefiting not just the child and family but all of society. When we let market forces prevail, the nation is deprived of the benefits of all young children receiving quality early childhood services and being better prepared to become more effectively functioning members of society.[22]

2. Child care is also a merit good: It provides more benefits to consumers than they realize, and as a result, consumers tend to buy less than they would if they fully realized care's benefits;[23] parents do not have adequate information about the quality options and the effect of optional programs on their children's development.

3. The child care field cannot resolve these problems alone. According to Helburn and her colleagues:

    Because of competitive conditions and the complex nature of [child care] services, it is difficult for many providers to improve services on their own unless they have access to unique resources. The market will fail to provide sufficient high-quality early childhood services if left to itself.[24]

The challenge for policy makers is to bridge the gap between what parents can afford and what quality costs. The critical question is when and how to intervene in the child care market.

REFERENCES

1. S. L. Hofferth, A. Brayfield, S. Deitch, and P. Holcomb, *The National Child Care Survey, 1990* (Washington, DC: The Urban Institute, 1991).

2. B. Willer, "Estimating the Full Cost of Quality," in B. Willer, ed., *Reaching the Full Cost of Quality in Early Childhood Programs* (Washington, DC: NAEYC, 1990), p. 61.

3. John Morris, University of Denver, July 1992. Personal comment at meeting of Committee for Economic Development, New York, NY, 1992.

4. R. R. Ruopp and J. Travers, "Janus Faces Day Care: Perspective on Quality and Cost," in E. F. Zigler and E. W. Gordon, eds., *Day Care: Scientific and Social Policy Issues* (Boston: Auburn House, 1982).

5. Louis Harris and Associates, Inc., *The Philip Morris Child Care Survey* (New York: Philip Morris Companies, 1989).

6. S. L. Hofferth et al., 1991.

7. S. L. Hofferth et al., 1991.

8. B. Willer, S. L. Hofferth, E. E. Kisker, P. Divine-Hawkins, E. Farquhar, and F. B. Glanz, *The Demand and Supply of Child Care in 1990* (Washington, DC: National Association for the Education of Young Children; U.S. Department of Health and Human Services, Administration on Children, Youth, and Families; U.S. Department of Education, Office of the Undersecretary, 1991).

9. S. L. Hofferth et al., 1991.

10. B. Willer, 1990, p. 24.

11. V. R. Fuchs and M. Coleman, "Small Children, Small Pay: Why Child Care Pays So Little," *The American Prospect* (Winter 1991), pp. 74–79.

12. U.S. Department of Commerce, Bureau of the Census, *Money Income of Households, Families and Persons in the United States*, Current Population Reports Series P-6, No. 162, Table 36 (Washington, DC: U.S. Government Printing Office, 1987).

13. B. Willer, 1990.

14. M. O'Connell, *Who's Minding the Kids*, U.S. Bureau of the Census Current Population Reports, Series P-70, No. 20, 10 (Washington, DC: Government Printing Office, 1987).

15. D. E. Friedman, *A Survey of Resource and Referral Agencies* (Washington, DC: National Association of Child Care Referral Agencies, 1989), p. 11.

16. G. Adams, *Who Knows How Safe?* (Washington, DC: Children's Defense Fund, 1990), p. vii.

17. G. Morgan, personal communication, January 1991.

18. M. Fried and M. Whitebook, *Innovative Approaches to the Salary Dilemma: The Massachusetts and Toronto Experiments* (Oakland, CA: Child Care Employee Project, 1989).

19. E. Marx and C. Zinsser, with T. Porter, *Raising Child Care Salaries and Benefits: An Evaluation of the New York State Salary Enhancement Legislations* (New York: Bank Street College and the Center for Public Advocacy Research, 1990).

20. G. Adams, 1990, p. vii.

21. S. W. Helburn, J. R. Morris, and M. Culkin, *The Costs of Child Care and Education* (Denver: Department of Economics, University of Colorado, 1991), p. 13.

22. M. L. Culkin, S. W. Helburn, and J. R. Morris, "Current Price Versus Full Cost: An Economic Perspective," in B. Willer, ed., *Reaching the Full Cost of Quality in Early Childhood Programs* (Washington, DC: NAEYC, 1990), p. 26.

23. M. L. Culkin et al., 1990.

24. M. L. Culkin et al., 1990, p. 16.

CHAPTER 5

The Response from
Government and Business

This chapter outlines the government's role in child care, reviews recent legislative initiatives, and examines employer involvement in improving the supply, accessibility, cost, and quality of child care.

GOVERNMENT'S ROLE IN CHILD CARE

The history of government involvement in child care reveals a patchwork of programs. At the turn of the century, day nurseries were established for low-income children. During the Depression, the Federal Emergency Relief Administration provided child care funds to alleviate economic hardship and to create child care jobs for the unemployed. Thousands of centers were established during World War II to promote female employment in war-related industries through funds provided by the Lanham Act.[1]

The 1970s saw five unsuccessful attempts to pass comprehensive child care legislation. Each failed because of political confrontations or moral ambiguities; for instance, President Nixon, at the same time that he was promoting his Family Assistance Plan, vetoed the overwhelmingly passed Comprehensive Child Development Act of 1971, likening child care to the Soviet style of child rearing. Then, the 1974 and 1975 Child and Family Services Acts were attacked by conservatives, echoing Nixon's fears that child care would lead to the destruction of the family. Simultaneously, a campaign to have public schools take control of child care caused enough infighting among child care constituents for Congress to abandon all hope for the bill's passage. Senator Cranston's Child Care Act of 1979, a more modest version of earlier bills, was never raised on the floor for a vote and died with less than a whimper.

Current Federal Spending

In 1988, the federal government invested less than $6.6 billion in child care, including both expenditures and lost income due to tax credits. This sum was less than 4 percent of total federal spending on education and social welfare, excluding health.[2] (See Figure 5.1.) Concealed in this figure is a dramatic shift over a period of years from a supply-side strategy (funds distributed directly to child care providers) to a demand-side strategy (funds distributed to parents through vouchers or the tax system). A 1987 study by the Congressional Budget Office concluded that although lower-income families would benefit more from supply-side subsidies, demand-side emphasis has meant that "a disproportionately larger share of federal child care dollars has been going to middle- and upper-income families in recent years,

Figure 5.1
FEDERAL SPENDING FOR CHILD CARE, 1977–1988

Program	Administering Agency	Federal Spending (Millions of Dollars)			
		1977	1980	1984	1988
Title XX (Social Services Block Grants)	Department of Health and Human Services	809	600	535	660
Head Start	Department of Health and Human Services	448	735	996	1,206
Area Economic and Human Resource Development Program	Appalachian Regional Commission	9	11	1	0
Child Care Food Program	Department of Agriculture	120	217	357	586
Job Training Partnership Act	Department of Labor	—	—	9	9
Aid to Families with Dependent Children (Work-Expense Disregard)	Department of Health and Human Services	84	60	35	44
Work Incentive Program	Department of Health and Human Services	57	115	13	9
Food Stamps (Dependent Care Deduction)	Department of Agriculture	35	35	35	50
Tax Exclusion for Employer-Provided Child Care	Internal Revenue Service	—	—	40	65
	Subtotal	1,562	1,773	2,021	2,629
	(1988 dollars)	(3,055)	(2,542)	(2,299)	(2,629)
Child Care Tax Credit	Internal Revenue Service	521	956	2,649	3,920
	Total	2,083	2,729	4,670	6,549
	(1988 dollars)	(4,061)	(3,912)	(5,312)	(6,549)

Source: P. K. Robins, "Federal Financing of Child Care: Alternative Approaches and Economic Implications," paper prepared for the "Economic Implications and Benefits of Child Care" conference (sponsored by Child Care Action Campaign, New York, NY): January 1988.

Note: Data are for the fiscal year except for the Child Care Tax Credit, which is measured over the calendar year.

and consequently there has been a growing inequity in the distribution of federal child care benefits."[3]

Although federal spending on child care has risen by almost 65 percent in constant dollars since 1977, to repeat—all of the increased benefits have been demand-side subsidies that have mostly benefited middle- and upper-income families. Excluding the Dependent Care Tax Credit, a demand-side subsidy for employed parents, federal spending for child care declined by almost 12 percent in constant dollars from 1977 to 1988. (Under the Federal Dependent Care Tax Credit, the maximum credit is 30 percent of allowable child care expenses for families with incomes of $10,000 or less; this decreases to 20 percent for families with incomes above $28,000. The most a family could claim against their taxes would be $720 for one child or $1,440 for two or more children.)

Robins points out that some demand-side subsidies restrict consumer choice.[4] For example, while in-home care is eligible under the Dependent Care Tax Credit, it is not generally eligible for subsidization under Title XX, Social Service block grant monies that can be used at state discretion for the funding of child care for income-eligible employed parents. Although Title XX funds are generally perceived as a strategy to fund child care suppliers, many states use the funds to distribute vouchers directly to parents. Title XX also has a mandated state match, so the states also contribute, in some cases substantially.

Stephan and Schillmoeller identified 22 separate federal programs for child care—a patchwork of uncoordinated programs that vary in purpose, eligibility requirements, type of service offered, and required standards.[5] Figure 5.1 presents the federal spending changes in ten of the largest child care programs between 1977 and 1988. In 1977, Title

XX accounted for the largest portion of federal spending on child care at close to 40 percent of the total. By 1988 this was down to about 10 percent — in constant dollars, a 60 percent decline. Over the same decade, the Dependent Care Tax Credit expanded significantly and by 1988 was the dominant form of government child care subsidy: It accounted for about 60 percent of all federal spending for child care — up from 25 percent in 1977.[6]

The passage of the Economic Recovery Tax Act of 1981, which made child care a nontaxable benefit, helped to shift federal policy toward demand-side subsidies over the past decade. This act prompted numerous employers to create a Flexible Spending Account (FSA) that included a Dependent Care Assistance Plan (DCAP), which allows employees to use pretax dollars on child care, and employers to "provide" financial assistance to their employees without assuming any costs except administrative and communication.[7] Companies also save money because they do not have to pay Social Security or unemployment taxes on the amount by which employees reduce their salaries through DCAPs.

DCAPs are essentially regressive, giving greater subsidies to higher-income families (with incomes over $25,000), while the Child Care Tax Credit is progressive. Because DCAPs are currently the most popular form of child care assistance provided by the business community and funded by the federal tax system, the failure of federal dollars to benefit lower-income families remains a central issue among policy makers.

Recent Developments in Federal Initiatives

The Family Support Act (FSA, though not the Flexible Spending Account mentioned above) was passed by Congress in 1988. It is expected to have a substantial impact on the child care system because it requires Aid to Families with Dependent Children (AFDC) or welfare mothers with children over age three — or over one year old, at the state's discretion — to work or to participate in job training at the same time it requires states to provide child care for these families. Preliminary evidence suggests that in some states with too few subsidized slots, most slots are being turned over to mothers receiving AFDC, which pushes other low-income families out of the subsidized system altogether.

Between 1987 and 1990, over 200 child care bills were introduced into Congress, and comprehensive child care legislation, the Child Care and Development Block Grant, was signed into law in November 1990. These measures were aimed at improving the quality, cost, and accessibility of child care (see Figure 5.2).

As this child care legislation was making its way through Congress, there was constant debate over one of the most difficult issues in child care: Whether national standards for child care quality should be established. As mentioned in previous chapters, while standards do not guarantee quality, children do receive better quality care and education in states with higher standards.[8] The National Governors' Association, however, opposed the idea, believing that each state should be able to determine the effect standards would have on the child care market. The Child Care and Development Block Grant Act did partially resolve the issue by requiring that states establish health and safety requirements — such as infectious disease prevention and control (including immunizations), building safety requirements, and health and safety training for providers — for all providers receiving public funds.

States may impose less stringent requirements on provid-

Figure 5.2

1990 FEDERAL CHILD CARE INITIATIVES

CHILD CARE AND DEVELOPMENT BLOCK GRANT

The 1990 block grant for child care provides states with the federal funds to address the issues of affordability, accessibility, and quality. The legislation authorizes $731 million for the block grant in FY 1991, $825 million in FY 1992, $925 million in FY 1993, and necessary sums for FY 1994 and 1995. States will receive funds according to a formula that takes into account the number of children younger than age five, and the number of children receiving free and reduced price school lunch, and state per capital income.

Child Care Services and Activities

- States must use three quarters of the new block grant to help families pay for child care or for activities to increase the supply or improve the quality of child care. However, the law does not require states to apportion funds between direct services and other activities in any particular way.
- Working parents are eligible for assistance if their children are younger than age thirteen and their family income is less than 75 percent of the state median income.
- States must offer eligible parents certificates to help pay for child care of their choice. States also may give providers grants or contracts to offer subsidized care.
- Parents receiving certificates may select any licensed, regulated, or registered provider. This includes care by relatives, family day care providers, religious institutions, and schools, as long as the provider complies with state and local law and meets minimal requirements set forth in the bill.

Activities to Improve Quality and Accessibility

- Twenty-five percent of the block grant is reserved for quality improvements and early childhood education and latchkey programs.
- States must use no less than 20 percent of the reserved funds for quality improvement activities. These may include: grants or loans to help providers meet state or local standards; activities to improve enforcement of state standards and licensing requirements; training and technical assistance; and improvement of salaries for child care providers.
- States must use no less than 75 percent of the reserved funds for early childhood education and latchkey programs. States will provide these services through grants and contracts. Areas eligible for concentration grants under the Chapter I education program will have priority for these services.

GRANTS TO STATES

Entitlement Funding for Child Care Services

States will receive a total of $300 million per year ($1.5 billion over five years) beginning in fiscal year 1991 to provide child care to families who need such care in order to work and would otherwise be at risk of becoming dependent on AFDC. Child care providers receiving funds would have to be licensed, regulated, or registered, except that no requirements would apply to care provided solely to family members. In addition $50 million per year beginning in fiscal year 1992 has been authorized (but not yet appropriated) to improve standards, monitor compliance with State standards, and provide training to providers. Half of these funds would be used for training.

continued

119

Figure 5.2—Continued

TAX CREDITS TO FAMILIES

- **Expansion of the Earned Income Tax Credit (EITC) For Low-Income Working Families with Children**

    Basic credit. Substantially increases the value of the earned income tax credit, which is an income subsidy for working families struggling to make ends meet, beginning in 1991. Also adjusts the credit for two family sizes. The projected maximum EITC in 1994 would be $1,852 for a family with one child and $2,013 for a family with two or more children, compared with $1,127 under current law for all family sizes. In addition, includes provisions designed to simplify administration of the credit. Equals $12.4 billion over five years.

    Supplemental credit for newborns. Provides an additional credit to families with a child under age one, beginning in 1991. The projected maximum credit for newborns would be $403 in 1994. Budget cost equals $.7 billion over five years. Eligible families could claim the supplemental credit or the dependent care tax credit, but not both.

- **New Tax Credit for Health Insurance Premiums for Families with Children**

    A refundable tax credit would be available beginning in 1991 to cover certain health insurance expenses of families with children. The projected maximum would be $483 in fiscal year 1994. Budget cost equals $5.2 billion over five years.

    Total cost: $19 billion over the five-year budget period.

Source: The Children's Defense Fund, October 31, 1990.

ers that do not receive government funds, though states that choose to relax their current regulations must explain their reasoning, and all states must conduct a one-time review of their licensing and regulatory policies. Whether this will be a problem or not remains unclear.

Under the act, some funds may be used to improve quality. However, the interim regulations of the act, issued in 1991, contradict this by stressing that nothing (i.e., quality efforts) should interfere with or diminish parental choice. Thus, quality enhancement, which was an important feature of the act itself, has been severely curtailed by current federal regulations.

Federal and State Initiatives
to Stimulate Business Involvement

Since employers began expressing interest in child care in the early 1980s, government may have focused more attention on ways to stimulate corporate support for child care than it has on constructing a child care framework business can build upon. For instance, 57 bills in 21 states have been introduced to provide tax credits to employers providing child care, and 13 states have passed tax credit legislation. However, while cost may seem to be a barrier to employer involvement, very few of these 13 states had any corporate takers.[9] There are numerous reasons for this lack of response from the business community, but chief among them is that most companies do not want to create new services as much as they want to help their employees find or pay for community-based programs. This requires a foundation of services laid down by government and community agencies, such as schools and churches.

EMPLOYER ROLES IN CHILD CARE

There is a considerably uneven distribution of employer-supported child care across the country, due to the fact that business investment in communities is highest where a strong system of child care already exists and lowest when there are no services in the community or the "system" is in crisis. Overall, business efforts have helped to increase the supply, improved access to services, helped to make child care more affordable, and enhanced the quality of existing programs.

In the past, the corporate community had a history of attending only sporadically to the child care needs of employees. The first child care centers sponsored by employers were created during the Civil War to help women join in the war effort. By 1910, the Association of Day Nurseries recorded the existence of 450 centers in working-class neighborhoods. Some of these nurseries were sponsored by the factories employing the children's mothers. And although some were innovative, others were known for their poor quality and unsanitary conditions, in some cases, no less oppressive than the factories themselves: "The rare industrial day nursery, funded by a mill or factory with a substantial number of female employees, [was not] necessarily more sanitary, better equipped and staffed than its neighborhood counterpart."[10]

The two World Wars gave rise to further rounds of employer-sponsored centers, and during World War II, employer-sponsored child care programs received support from the federal government. In 1940, Congress passed the Lanham Act, and a year later, to help the war effort, passed amendments that encouraged the creation of community-based child care programs in defense plant areas. Many of the centers set up during this period both had innovative educational and care practices, as well as support for working mothers — such as laundry and hot dinners sent home with the children.

After the war, industry's interest in child care lay dormant until the 1960s. In 1967, legislation provided an opportunity for rapid tax amortization of constructed buildings used to serve employees' children. The increasing labor force participation of women and a climate of social responsibility prompted about 18 companies to experiment with on-site centers. Most of these centers closed, due more to the failure of the companies than of the centers. During the 1970s, employer-supported child care was referred to as a "miniature curiosity," and it was predicted that it would never "become a significant factor in the American day care landscape."[11]

Current Employer Interest in Child Care

Employer-supported child care is far more than a miniature curiosity today. Business investments in the field have dramatically changed the child care landscape in numerous communities around the country. The number of employers with child care programs has increased from 600 employers with child care programs in 1982 to an estimated 5,600 in 1990—a dramatic change, though it still represents only 13 percent of the 44,000 U.S. employers with more than 100 employees (see Figure 5.3).

Currently, there are several obstacles to employer involvement in child care, ranging from attitudes to fiscal constraints to lack of information. Among the most common concerns of companies are:

Work and family life should remain separate. Companies have traditionally designed their cultures around the idea that "employees should keep their personal problems at home." In this culture, family needs are considered outside the purview of business, any attempts to address such needs are considered unnecessary interference, and work and family life are seen as separate worlds.[12] But as the composition of our labor force continues to change, many employees will not al-

Figure 5.3

GROWTH OF EMPLOYER-SUPPORTED CHILD CARE

Number of Companies

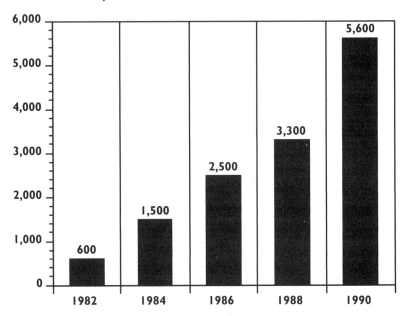

Source: D. E. Friedman, "Update on Employer-Supported Child Care," distributed memo, Families and Work Institute, 1991.

ways be able to leave their personal problems at home, mostly because there will be no one there to take care of them.

Child care creates equity problems. Companies are often concerned that when supporting child care, they are serving only women employees. Management may not see that child care affects both parents. It also may fear that if it provides child care assistance, employees who are not parents will demand a benefit of equal value. Many employers providing child care support, however, have not found this to be the case. In fact, there have been reports of CEOs' receiving letters of gratitude for introducing a child care program from nonparents who are pleased to be working for the kind of company that would provide this service. Other non-parents are relieved that their coworkers are receiving the company's assistance in securing high-quality, stable child care arrangements. Still, corporate needs assessments conducted by the Families and Work Institute do show that some employees—less than 5 percent—resent the company's attention to parents' needs.

Child care poses dangerous liability risks. In our litigious society, employers fear liability suits from employees whose children use the company's child care programs. Up to the present, very few cases have been brought to court, and most issues have arisen out of the normal trip-and-fall occurrences in an on-site center. A recent report from the Department of Labor, requested by President Bush to determine the degree to which liability and liability insurance concerns prevent employers from creating child care programs, concluded:

> We believe that there is currently no significant impediment to obtaining or affording child care liability insurance for employers who wish to provide on-site or near-site child care. However, there is clearly a perception among those employers who do not provide child care services that potential liability, if not liability insurance, represents a serious drawback in their

125

consideration to establish on-site or near-site child care centers. . . . The more involved an employer stays in the operation of a center, the greater the emphasis on the quality of the child care program and risk reduction. For companies that own and operate child care centers, risk is often handled as a "quality" issue; [causing them to develop] a child care center and program designed to prevent accidents from occurring, thereby reducing liability risk.[13]

In general, the quality of company-sponsored child care centers is superior to that of community-based programs, and this may be due, in large part, to company concerns about liability and the program's expected visibility.

An on-site child care center is the only option. With so much attention focused on the on-site center, many employers with reasons for not creating an on-site center do not explore other options. As described below, however, there are many ways an employer can make a difference in the quality of their employees' child care, such as providing information on child care to employees and working with community-based programs.

Child care costs too much. While it is true that an on-site child care center is an expensive option, there are other far less expensive options, described below, for companies that want to provide child care support to employees.

These perceived obstacles to employer involvement in child care are gradually eroding as more employers publicize their positive experiences with child care and describe the payoffs child care support has reaped for the company.

Stages of Employer-Supported Child Care

The evolution of employer-supported child care has three stages:

Stage I. Companies overcome their initial resistance and introduce one (or two) child care initiatives. This strategy is seen as separate and distinct from any other human resource issue facing the firm. There is no systematic investigation of how company characteristics (such as work schedules or travel requirements) might also contribute to child care problems. Any task force formed at this stage is generally called the "child care task force" and its mission is "single-issue," as are the solutions generated.

Stage II. Companies reaching this stage realize that the piecemeal approach is not effective. The task force is now called the "work and family task force," based on the underlying assumption that all employees feel some tension between their jobs and home responsibilities, whether they are married or single, parents, or nonparents. A more senior-level commitment from the company develops, and a champion who is deeply committed to the issue is often given the job of shepherding the development of recommendations and the imple-

127

mentation of more comprehensive policies and programs.

Stage III. Whereas efforts to tackle the more complex issues of work schedules and company culture often begin in Stage II, they become core elements in Stage III. Management training designed to sensitize managers to work-family issues and to the resolution of work-family problems may be instituted. The emphasis is on ensuring implementation of new policies and programs, developing flexibility within the corporate environment, and linking work-family issues to the business strategy as well as to other human resource issues, such as managing diversity, developing human capital, or improving quality. (See Figure 5.4.)

Among the 188 companies surveyed by the Families and Work Institute, 33 percent are in Pre-Stage I. In other words, they are not yet involved in work-family issues in any way. Forty-six percent of the companies surveyed are in Stage I, while 19 percent are in Stage II, and only two percent are in Stage III.

The companies that have begun this three-stage process have primarily been large corporations in high-growth industries. The industries most likely to be family-friendly are computers, commercial banking and life insurance, diversified financial companies, and pharmaceuticals. An analysis of the predictors of developing such policies revealed that companies that have recently undergone some corporate change (such as downsizing, merger, or acquisition) were most responsive. Having more females or being unionized were not significant.[15] Concerns about the economic health of many unionized manufacturing companies

Figure 5.4

EVOLUTION OF EMPLOYER
WORK-FAMILY PROGRAMS

Stage I: Developing a Programmatic Response	Stage II: Developing an Integrated Approach	Stage III: Changing the Culture
Commitment		
Emerging but Tentative	**Work-Family as a Human Resource Issue**	**Work-Life as a Competitive Issue**
Overcoming assumptions: • Work-family is not a business issue • Equity means the same policy for all employees • Work-family is a woman's issue • Child care assistance means creating on- or near-site facilities	• Focus on child care is expanded to include other work-family issues (elder care, relocation, etc.) • Programs and policies broaden	• Work-family issues throughout the company are integrated with such issues as gender equity and diversity • There is movement toward a life-cycle approach, thus broadening the concept of work-family to "work-life" • Company involvement extends to global issues and concerns • Developing work-family policies is seen as a continuous, dynamic, problem-solving process
Process		
Identifying the Problem	**Centralizing Responsibility for Work-Family Programs**	**Mainstreaming the Issues**
• Committed individual(s)/ champion(s) takes on the job of making a business case for a company response to work-family issues • Champion(s) convinces others that there is a cost to not responding, e.g.: employees may miss time or be less productive because of unmet child care needs • Champion(s) demonstrates many possible solutions • If a task force is created to assess employees' needs (usually through surveys or focus groups), its focus is on child care	• Part- or full-time responsibility is assigned to an individual or group, often at the level of director, manager or vice president • Position of work-family coordinator may be instituted • Top-level commitment begins to emerge • Work-family initiatives are seen as a key to recruiting and retaining skilled employees • Training to help supervisors manage work-family issues may be initiated • If a task force is created, its focus is on work-family issues	• Implementing flexible time and leave policies becomes central • Changing the workplace to be more flexible calls traditional work assumptions into question • Work-family management training is undertaken, or such training is integrated into core management education programs • If a task force is created, its focus is on work-life issues

continued

Figure 5.4—Continued

Stage I: Developing a Programmatic Response	Stage II: Developing an Integrated Approach	Stage III: Changing the Culture
Solution		
One at a Time	**Integrated**	**Holistic and Strategic**
• Programs generally focus on child care for employees with young children • Separate solutions are found in the following areas: child care assistance, flexible time policies and flexible benefits • The one or two solutions developed are seen as an add-on to other human resource programs	• The extent to which personnel policies, time and leave policies, and benefits affect family life is considered • A package of several policies and programs is developed in response to a wide variety of work-family problems • Policies are periodically reviewed and revised • Work-family and other issues are seen as ongoing and dynamic	• Full consideration is given to company culture and its effect on family/personal life • Consideration is given to the effects of using family-responsive policies on career development • Work-family issues become linked to strategic business planning
Community Focus		
Information Sharing	**Collaborative**	**Influential**
• Companies begin to share information with each other, but generally act alone to solve problems and develop programs	• Companies and individuals come together to share information, solve problems and develop joint solutions • Companies and individuals reach out to their communities to share resources • Some advocacy for local, state and federal programs such as Head Start	• Companies advocate, or designate funds for improving the quality and supply of community-based dependent care services • Company programs reach out to the underserved in their communities as well as their own employees

Source: E. Galinsky, D. E. Friedman, C. A. Hernandez, *The Corporate Reference Guide to Work-Family Programs* (New York: Families and Work Institute, 1991), p. 10.

130

have preempted attention from the child care dimension of human resources. This profile, however, may change now that unions have begun to adopt child care and work-family concerns as part of their agenda. Also, because unions now want to attract more members, particularly new white-collar workers and women, work-family issues are more likely to appear on the bargaining table.

The Range of Corporate Initiatives to Improve Child Care

Corporate child care efforts may address all aspects of services, supply, cost, or quality. The kind of initiative undertaken usually depends on the particular inadequacies of the surrounding community's child care market. And employers may act alone, or work in collaboration with other employers, community agencies, or government agencies (see California Child Care Initiative Project, Maryland Shareholders, and One Small Step case studies).

Increasing Supply

The number of **on- or near-site child care centers** continues to grow. Figures 5.3 and 5.5 show 5,600 employers providing some form of child care support and approximately 1,400 doing so by sponsoring a child care center, or 13 percent of large companies.[16]

Most of the centers (900) are sponsored by hospitals, 250 are sponsored by government agencies, and another 250 by corporations. The recent growth in on-site centers is due largely to developers' placing child care centers in office parks as an amenity to attract companies, as well as to government agencies, which often create multiple centers.

Figure 5.5
ESTIMATED PREVALENCE OF VARIOUS CHILD CARE OPTIONS PROVIDED BY EMPLOYERS

Option		Estimated Number
On- or Near Site Centers		1,400
by Hospitals	900	
by Corporations	250	
by Government	250	
Family child care, school-age care and sick child care		100
Resource and referral services		1,500
Discounts, vouchers		100
Dependent Care Assistance Plans in flexible benefits		2,500
		5,600

Source: The Families and Work Institute, 1991.

Some sponsors work in consortium arrangements, sharing the costs, risks, and benefits of having a high-quality center conveniently located for employees. Some create centers and a network of family child care homes (see America West 24-Hour Center and Family Day Care Network case study).

The on-site center is not feasible for most employers. Many firms are too small; they lack the resources to finance a center, and a labor pool large enough to fill it. The commuting patterns of employees and the costs of downtown space make it difficult for companies in large urban areas to create centers that employees want to use or can afford. Other work sites, such as chemical plants, may be inappropriate for children.

As an alternative, some firms have tried to increase the supply of care by focusing on **family child care initiatives** — neighborhood arrangements in the private home of the provider, where younger children (under age three) are

132

most often cared for. American Express, for instance, funds family child care associations and resource and referral agencies to recruit and train new family child care homes and help them become licensed. Mervyn's and Target Stores, subsidiaries of Dayton Hudson, have devoted almost $10 million for a multiyear effort to increase the supply of high-quality family child care homes in the more than 30 communities in which they have stores (see Mervyn's, Target Stores, and Dayton Hudson Family-to-Family Project case study).

After-school care is another concern of parents, and therefore of growing concern to companies. Millions of children return to empty homes at the end of the day and many parents have no access to telephones to make sure they are safely at home. Some companies have set up a **phone-in service** so that older children can call when they arrive home or when they need assistance or someone to talk to. (Companies and child care experts agree that young children—in elementary school—should not be left home alone.) Other companies offer **after-school services** as part of their on-site child care centers or help create such services in schools, YWCAs, and other community agencies (see Coors Brewing Company After-School Initiative case study).

Recently, companies have become concerned about absenteeism due to parents' staying home with sick children. Some firms have created **sick child care centers** or **emergency family child care homes** to care for mildly ill or recuperating children (see IDS Sick Child Care Program case study). Others, such as a group of New York City companies, have developed an in-home nursing service that sends trained providers into the child's home in an emergency (see Emergency Child Care Service—New York City case study). The success of these new initiatives has varied, since parents may be unwilling to bring their sick children to a strange location, and others may be reluctant to have a stranger come into their home.

Because some companies have realized that parents may want to stay—and should stay—with very sick children, they are revising their sick leave policies to permit employees to do so. One advantage of this policy is that workers stop lying about the reason for their absence, admitting that it is their children, and not they, who are ill.

A recent Conference Board survey of 521 large companies found that 58 percent of large companies offer sick family leave (59 percent of it unpaid).[17] The 1990 survey of 188 Fortune 1000 companies found that fewer than 5 percent had specifically designated family, sick, or emergency days.[18] This leave is typically one or two days added to existing sick leave policy, or the permission to use sick leave for family purposes. More common is the use of personal leave (offered by 77 percent of large companies) or family leave (offered by 16 percent of large companies).[19]

Providing Access and Information

About 300 **child care resource and referral** agencies around the country help parents shorten their search time for care and become wiser consumers of the care they purchase. About 1,500 companies contract with these agencies locally to provide counseling and referrals to employees. Overall, 55 percent of Fortune 1000 companies offer child care resource and referral services to their employees.[20] In 1984, IBM became the first company to offer its employees access to a nationwide network of referral services. As of 1991, over 70 national corporations have followed suit (see

Lincoln National Life Insurance Resource and Referral Program case study). Most employers who provide this service also contribute funds to the referral agencies for the development of new services. For example, these efforts have contributed to the development of an estimated 12,000 to 15,000 providers per year since 1984, most of which are family child care homes.

Companies also provide information to employees through **parenting seminars**, **caregiver fairs**, **employee support groups**, **handbooks**, **videos**, **parent resource libraries**, and **work and family newsletters**. Some firms have expanded their employee assistance programs (EAPs) to include a wide range of family issues.

Offsetting Costs

To help parents meet the cost of care, some employers contract with local centers for a **discount** for their employees. Others provide **vouchers**, enabling employees to choose from a wider range of programs (see Beneficial Management Corporation's Voucher Program and NationsBank's Voucher Program case studies). The amount of subsidy depends on the employee's family income, and is usually limited to incomes below $30,000. Retail chains and firms in other service industries have begun to take a renewed interest in vouchers because of the difficulty they have recruiting female labor. Since women are often at the lower end of the pay scale, they are likely to benefit less from a flexible benefits plan than they are from vouchers.

The **Dependent Care Assistance Plan (DCAP)** as part of a Flexible Spending Account (FSA) remains the most popular child care option for companies, and by 1990, 50 percent of *Fortune* 1000 companies had established FSAs.[21]

The DCAP enables employees to use up to $5,000 of pretax dollars to purchase child care services, but they have restrictions. Employees can use either an FSA or the IRS Dependent Care Tax Credit, or a combination of the two, but the *total* amount claimed must not exceed the amount allowed for the tax credit. Also, in order to get the tax benefit, employees must report the Social Security number of their caregiver. Unfortunately, many caregivers in the informal care market prefer not to claim this income and refuse to give out their Social Security numbers. Furthermore, if the funds in the account are not used up by the end of the year, they must be forfeited.

Beyond Employees: Helping the Community to Improve Supply and Quality

A growing number of companies have learned that state licensing standards provide only a minimum floor of health and safety protection, that state licensing laws do not necessarily provide quality care, and that a licensed program may not even be safe where enforcement efforts are minimal. In response to this problem, several forward-thinking companies are working with the National Association for the Education of Young Children accreditation program mentioned throughout this book, mostly by paying the several-hundred-dollar accreditation fees for programs in communities in which they have employees. In addition, a few companies are sponsoring training for family child care providers on three levels, according to Gwen Morgan: apprentice, competent provider, and master provider.[22]

Companies also stimulate the supply of quality care when they use child care resource and referral contracts, particularly through national contracts. At the same time as they are providing referrals, agencies receive funding from companies to provide training, follow-up, and monitoring of caregivers, and can help to ensure that state standards are met by more programs.

Stage II and Stage III companies in particular tend to look beyond the needs of their own employees and become involved in efforts to improve the quantity and quality of child care in the broader communities where they employ workers. For instance, IBM and AT&T have each created "funds" whose general purpose is to expand the supply of quality dependent care (see case studies). AT&T's Family Care Development Fund is spending $15 million between 1993 and 1995 on both child care and elder care. The Fund evolved during union negotiations and is designed to engage more union and management employees in actively assessing employee needs and community resources.

The IBM Child Care Resource and Development Fund will disburse $25 million over a five-year period for child care and elder care, $22 million of which is for child care. The administering agency, Work/Family Directions, has conducted needs assessments in primary IBM locations and determined where the child care system most needs assistance. Requests for proposals then target these specific needs in the identified communities (see IBM Funds for Dependent Care Initiatives and AT&T Family Care Development Fund case studies).

Collaborative Efforts to Expand and Improve Child Care

Other companies, operating in a single location, have pooled resources to address a variety of child care problems. In Charlotte, North Carolina, Duke Power CEO Bill Lee initiated the development of Corporate Champions (see case study). Nineteen Charlotte employers put forward $300,000 for distribution to local agencies to expand services and improve quality. An experiment begun by United Way in Minneapolis, Success by 6®, to have community leaders work together to ensure that children enter school as successes, is now operating or being developed in 24 communities, and being considered by another 31 (see case study). Small businesses are also involved, through such organizations as Kiwanis International (see case study).

The 1992 announcement of the American Business Collaboration for Quality Dependent Care heralds a new level of community involvement. It is an effort of 137 employers in 44 communities to increase the supply of quality services for their employers (see case study).

Advocacy

A few companies have taken on an advocacy role and attempted to work with government in the design of public policy. For instance, Mervyn's testified in support of federal child care standards. Other companies have joined with leaders from the public and voluntary sectors to create governors' or mayors' task forces that define problems and devise solutions. Important child care improvements in Tennessee, Illinois, New York, and Virginia can be attributed to corporate participation in such task forces. A stronger corporate voice in Washington and in governors' offices also would help government to be more effective in its own efforts to involve business in child care.

Some companies have recognized the importance of generating public support for child care through research, conferences, and most often, the media. American Express, in conjunction with PBS, sponsored a teleconference just before the airing of the documentary *Child Care America*. Philip Morris hired Louis Harris and Associates to conduct a national opinion poll on child care, which found that more than half the respondents were willing to have their tax dollars spent on an improved child care system.[23] Philip Morris also sponsored a teleconference and a media tour to publicize its findings.

CASE STUDIES

California Child Care Initiative Project (CCIP)

The California Child Care Initiative Project (CCIP) was developed in 1985 to address the shortage of licensed quality child care in California communities. Developed by the BankAmerica Foundation and funded by a public/private partnership of 33 organizations (10 public agencies and 23 private funders), the program relies on existing resource and referral agencies to recruit and train family child care providers. Since the program began, over 200 funders have contributed $5.4 million. CCIP was originally administered by the BankAmerica Foundation, but the San Francisco Foundation now acts as the fiscal intermediary. The California Child Care Resource and Referral Network, a statewide support group, manages and monitors the day-to-day activities of the Initiative.

During the 1986 year-long pilot project, six resource and referral agencies in five California counties successfully tested a process of supply building. Pilot goals were exceeded by 20 percent with the licensing of over 230 new family child care homes and the start-up of

139

five after-school programs. By the end of the CCIP's first year, over 1,100 new child care spaces had been created.

In the seven years from the pilot to the replication stage, the CCIP has generated 3,500 new licensed family day care providers and over 14,000 child care spaces. Over 20,000 new and experienced providers have been trained in delivering quality child care programs. In 1990, the Ford Foundation selected and funded the Michigan 4C Association and the Oregon Child Care Initiative to replicate California's successes. Their programs are adapted to the particular needs and circumstances of their funders, communities, and child care systems. Local sites have been selected and supply building activities are underway.

One county's success with the project was evaluated in 1987. Among 168 new family caregivers, 67 were recruited, trained, and licensed through the efforts of the Initiative. The study found that the CCIP-trained providers were more likely to join the local family child care association, participate in the Child Care Food Program, use book-lending services and borrow toys and equipment offered by the agency, as well as to seek additional training.

In 1992, the CCIP launched a demonstration phase to recruit and train Spanish-speaking family day care providers. Nine agencies throughout California were funded to increase the supply of such care. To support agencies' training efforts, the CCIP also developed new publications targeted for Spanish-language individuals. •

Maryland Shareholders

The Maryland Employers Advisory Council on Child Care, a select group of Maryland's corporate, union, and government leadership, was formed in January 1988 to see whether, by applying their professional insights and skills, they could find some new approaches to the child care crisis. The council was initiated as part of a project of the Maryland Committee for Children that was funded by the Morris Goldseker Foundation of Maryland, Inc., and the Aaron Straus and Lillie Straus Foundation, Inc. Sanford I. Weill, President, Chairman, and Chief Executive Officer of Commercial Credit Group Inc., agreed to head the group. His reason for doing so was, "Essentially, it is in the business community's self-interest to concern itself with the child care issue. In the long term, addressing the needs of children is an investment in our society's future."

After engaging in six months of intensive meetings and research, the council created a statewide plan recognizing the interests of the various shareholders in the child care delivery system, as well as parents, caregivers, employers, unions, governments, and civic, charitable, and advocacy organizations. Named the Maryland Child Care Resource Center Network, the plan is designed to reach to the roots of the present system. The core component of the network is the Child Care Resource Center (CCRC), designed to stimulate the supply, enhance the quality, and increase the accessibility of local child care resources through a range of activities. These include recruitment and continuing training of providers, technical assistance to employers and child care programs, resource and referral counseling, parenting education, data collection, and community education.

Each CCRC is linked, coordinated, and assisted by a statewide Child Care Resource Center. The model has been tested in three geographical areas over a three-year demonstration period at a cost of approximately $4,826,000 (funded primarily by state government and corporate and community philanthropy). Just under $1 million of the total was raised from the private sector by the business community. The network has successfully demonstrated its effectiveness and the State of Maryland has renewed its contract with the Maryland Committee for Children, Inc., to operate the network for another three years.

Sanford Weill says, "If our country is to grow and prosper, we have to have the facilities to take care of our children. And the corporate sector, as good citizens, ought to be the leaders to help create those services." •

One Small Step: The Bay Area Employer Child Care Coalition

In 1986, One Small Step (initially known as the Bay Area Employer Child Care Coalition) was convened by United Way of the Bay Area to help local employers address child care issues in the workplace. The initial objective of the coalition's founders — a group of 15 public and private sector representatives — was to educate local employers about the wide range of policy and program options available to meet the needs of both employees and businesses. In order to join the coalition, Bay Area employers made a commitment to take at least "one small step" to address the child care needs of their employees. The rationale for building a membership association was to provide employers in the community with a regular forum to exchange information, experiences, and strategies.

The One Small Step Coalition has been a great success in the Bay Area. Today, its membership has grown to almost 100 employers. In 1992, affiliate memberships were introduced, consisting of select service providers, consultants, labor representatives, university faculty, public policy advocates, and research professionals. The scope has also been expanded to include other "work and family" issues (e.g., members are now addressing elder care as well as child care issues). A majority of participating employers have instituted family-supportive programs such as dependent care flexible spending accounts, family leave policies, regular part-time work schedules, flextime policies, and a wide variety of informational assistance in the form of brochures, resource libraries, lunchtime seminars, and resource fairs. Growing numbers of employers in the coalition are also initiating job-share arrangements, telecommuting programs, compressed work weeks, resource and referral programs, and training for managers to sensitize them to the needs of working families.

The coalition is primarily funded by annual membership dues, in addition to assistance provided by United Way of the Bay Area. •

America West 24-Hour Center
and Family Day Care Network

Airline employees have greatly varied work schedules from month to month. When one employee proposed to top management the idea of 24-hour care, the idea was warmly received, particularly by the CEO, who was also a parent. The company care began by funding the expansion of family child care in the community and saw the center care as an extension of that effort.

The home-based component of the program consists of 50 homes in the Phoenix area, and eight in Las Vegas. Providers must receive training in child development and emergency care. They are carefully screened, including fingerprinting, an FBI background check, and home safety inspection. America West also sponsors a toy lending library that can be rotated among the homes. Providers also receive reduced-rate flight passes.

In 1989, 13 centers in the Phoenix area were made available to America West employees through an agreement with Sunrise Preschools. One of these is open 24 hours a day. The fees vary, but the company provides a 25 to 50 percent subsidy depending on the total family income of the employee. Care is subsidized by America West for work-related hours only. Employees may also set aside tax dollars for their child care expenses. The child care program has generated considerable local, state, and national attention. It received a "Pioneer Award" from the Child Care Challenge sponsored by the U.S. Congress.

Plans are underway to expand the center-based and the home-based care program, as employee need and usage expand. America West ultimately plans to develop child care programs for all cities that the airline serves and currently has center affiliations in 15 America West cities. Subsidy is available at centers accredited by the National Association for the Education of Young Children in five cities as part of a pilot program. •

Mervyn's, Target Stores and Dayton Hudson's Family-to-Family Project

The Family-to-Family Project was launched in 1988 by the Dayton Hudson Foundation and Mervyn's. Target Stores joined in 1990. Over a seven-year period, these three entities will invest almost $7 million to increase the quality of family child care in 32 communities across the United States. The goal of the Family-to-Family is not to increase the supply of family child care, but to improve the quality of the existing supply.

The funding organizations have identified one organization to sponsor the project in each community. Usually the organization is a child care resource and referral agency (R&R), but in some cases it is a community college, vocational-technical school, or family child care provider association. In 1991, the average grant to sponsoring organizations was $216,000 over a three-year period. In return, each site:

• Offers a training course of at least 15 hours to an average of 90 family child care providers per year if the project has just one site, and 210 providers per year if the project has multiple sites.

145

- Implements an accreditation program in the community, and helps an average of five providers become accredited per year.

- Helps create or strengthen local provider associations.

- Conducts consumer education activities.

Additionally, the Dayton Hudson Foundation, Mervyn's, and Target Stores are investing almost $3 million in a national public education campaign, Child Care Aware. The purpose of this effort is to give the local sites technical assistance and additional funds for public education.

In 1990, the Dayton Hudson Foundation contracted with the Families and Work Institute to conduct a three-year evaluation of the Family-to-Family Project. The goals of the evaluation are to examine the impact of the project at local, state, and national levels. Finally, the evaluation will examine lessons learned across the sites and identify successful strategies for replication in a publication that will be made available to the child care community. •

Coors Brewing Company After-School Initiative

A survey conducted with a random sample of 500 Coors employees in 1987 indicated the need for before- and after-school services among 52 percent of employees who returned the survey. Smaller, but significant, numbers needed care for infants, toddlers, preschoolers, and children thirteen or older. The needs assessment identified three major parental concerns: the logistics of getting a child to school and back during the employee's workday, concern over the child's safety, and the difficulty of finding appropriate child care for older children. A metro-Denver and Jefferson County study created further concern within the company. This study found increases in alcohol consumption, rates of venereal disease, pregnancies, "dropout rates," and suicides among local teens.

Coors joined forces with the PTA of Jefferson County to develop plans for the expansion of before- and after-school child care to as many of the county's elementary and junior high schools as possible.

To date, Coors' contributions include:

- Hosting a kickoff conference of 200 community leaders

- Assigning a staff person to act as a liaison for the project

- Publicizing and disseminating information about the initiative and school-age child care (why it's needed, how to get a program started, etc.)

- Assisting principals and parent groups in conducting a needs assessment in their school community

- Making corporate space available to the community agencies involved in the initiative for the purpose of joint training for caregivers

- Contributing funds for scholarships for caregiver training

- Raising funds for program enhancement activities such as math and sciences enrichment

- Raising funds for scholarships for children in low-income families

Through the efforts of the initiative, the number of schools with school-age child care programs has increased from 12 to 50 elementary schools, the school district has adopted a school-age child care policy stating its support in the development of such programs, and the district has become a provider of school-age child care programs along with the local YMCAs, recreation districts, community college, and private for-profit and nonprofit center operators. •

IDS Sick Child Care Program

In 1987, the Work and Family Committee of IDS Financial Services, a subsidiary of American Express, began to investigate what local companies were doing to assist their employees. They also surveyed their employees, asking how many days were missed due to their children's sicknesses and how satisfied they were with their present sick child care arrangements. They discovered that 50 percent of employees with children missed between one and four days a year because of sick children.

The program began in July 1988. IDS contracted with three providers to provide trained caregivers in the children's own homes. IDS also contracted with two providers of center-based sick child care. The centers cost

$50 to $75 per day; the in-home services cost $14 per hour. IDS pays 75 percent of the costs; employees pay 25 percent.

When the program started, representatives from both services offered informational sessions at IDS. The parents are responsible for making contact with the agencies to arrange for care. After each use, the parent completes an evaluation form for IDS. This helps the company keep informed about how well the programs are meeting employees' needs. The programs also send IDS a monthly report on who used the services. Satisfaction has been high among users. IDS has found that 2.6 days is the average length of usage, indicating that it is for short-term crisis situations. •

Emergency Child Care Service — New York City

A group of seven New York City companies worked with Child Care, Inc., a private, nonprofit child care resource and referral agency, to found an emergency child care service in New York City. Emergency situations include times when: (1) a child is mildly ill; (2) a caregiver for a child is unavailable; (3) a child care program or school is not in session, but parents have to work; and (4) regular child care plans fall through for some other unforeseen reason. A feasibility study conducted by the consortium anticipated that the service would be used by 2 percent of the work force for an average of two consecutive days. Each company wholly or partially subsidizes the cost for its employees.

After slightly more than a year of study and planning, in September 1989, seven companies — Con Edison, HBO,

National Westminster Bank, Skadden Arps, Time Inc., Ernst and Young, and Colgate-Palmolive — launched a one-year pilot program. Each paid an administrative fee to Child Care, Inc., to coordinate the program and provide ongoing evaluation and research.

The companies, through Child Care, Inc., contract with home health care agencies serving the metropolitan area: New York City, Long Island, Westchester, southern Connecticut, and ten counties in New Jersey. These agencies have been cooperative in meeting employees' needs, including trying to provide the same caregiver to the same families. These agencies also have very high standards: caregivers must have 60 to 90 hours of training, 30 hours of observation in the field, have experience working with children, and solid work experience with their agency.

Each company has established its own rate of reimbursement for their employees. Some pay the whole cost of the approximately $13 per hour fee; others pay partial costs.

As expected, utilization has been low, but users have been overwhelmingly positive, as shown by repeat usage of close to 50 percent. Most requests are for child care breakdowns rather than sick child care, and professional staff have used the service more than other employees have. Many communities are watching New York to see how this experiment works. Since its inception, eight additional companies have joined the New York group. •

Lincoln National Life Insurance
Resource and Referral Program

As one of the few company in-house referral services,
Lincoln National's has met with enormous success. The
service is geared to both sides of the child care equation:
parents and providers. The program began in 1984 after
a group of employees approached the CEO about their
child care problems. Several parents then created a child
care task force to assess employee needs, review the
efforts of their competitors, and recommend new policies
and programs to management.

Resource and referral was selected as the initial option
because it was easy to start and because employees were
located at many sites. Lincoln National, as a leader in the
community, also wanted to see how best to utilize
existing community resources. It took about one year to
implement the program. The biggest problem was the
lack of available providers.

As a result, a major component of the program is the
recruitment of new providers. Family child care providers
who participate in Lincoln National's resource and
referral network are phone-screened and visited on-site.
They have an opportunity to participate in a minimum of
a three-hour training session, including one training
session that takes place in and showcases a family day
care provider's home. They also organize support groups
for the providers, and encourage them to participate in
professional organizations and to attend conferences. A
profile of all licensed centers, preschool programs, and
kindergartens is included on the referral list.

In addition to referrals, the company offers a summer

day camp, an annual family focus fair, child care assistance during job-related travel, emergency care and backup services, and three lunchtime seminar series: one seminar/support group for parents of children ages zero to three; one "family matters" seminar for parents of school-age children; and one series for employees who are concerned with elder care issues. Lincoln National also puts out a bimonthly newsletter called *Heir Care* that has over 1,600 subscribers, including employees and caregivers.

The service is run by the Department of Human Resources, and costs Lincoln National approximately $70,000 per year, including the salary of the coordinator. ●

Beneficial Management Corporation's Voucher Program

In the early 1980s, Beneficial considered a variety of child care options. The chairman of the board, himself a parent, was aware of the changing demographics of the work force and the kinds of stresses generated by work-family responsibilities. He wanted the company to assist its employees in some way and create a group to investigate various options.

After ruling out an on-site child care center due to the small number of employees who worked at headquarters, and concerns about cost, liability, and low usage, they settled on the voucher program. As Vice President of Human Resources, Lawrence Cole, Jr., said, "This would help employees where they wanted it most — in their pocketbooks."

Vouchers are available to all full-time and regular part-time employees who have been with Beneficial and its subsidiaries for six months. Since its inception in 1986, Beneficial has provided a flat amount of $60 per month per child with a maximum of $720 per year per child, or prorated for regular, part-time employees. The child must be enrolled in an accredited child care center, registered family child care home, or handicapped facility on a full-time basis. The child could be age zero to six: up to and including kindergarten. The employee and the facility must fill out an application for reimbursement, and receipts must be submitted to the company. The subsidy is paid out twice a year. There has been positive feedback from users. •

NationsBank's Voucher Program

CEO Hugh McColl has been the moving force behind NationsBank's progressive work-family initiatives. In 1986, the company surveyed its work force to learn about their work-family needs. The company created a resource and referral program that achieved the desired effects of increased appreciation and morale and reduced stress around finding child care. Feedback from the referral service also indicated that the cost of child care was a big problem.

NationsBank began a pilot subsidy program in January 1990 known as Child Care Plus. Its purpose is to promote quality, affordable care, and to help NationsBank attract and retain a capable work force.

Payments are available to employees with children under thirteen years old who are in care arrangements, if their parent's taxable income is $29,000 or less per year for single parents, $24,000 or less per year for married employees, as long as their annual gross income does not exceed $35,000. The limit was selected so that families who do not benefit from the NationsBank's Care Reimbursement Account would benefit from the new initiative.

Having determined that the average cost of child care in the Southeast is $50 to $90 per child per week, the company chose $70 per week as the basis for calculating the subsidy. In order to promote quality, the subsidy rate varies depending on whether the care used is licensed. Employees are reimbursed up to $35 per week maximum for licensed care and $20 per week for legal, but unlicensed care. •

IBM Funds for Dependent Care Initiatives

In November 1989, IBM announced the IBM Funds for Dependent Care Initiatives — a $25 million effort to address the child care and elder care needs of IBM employees in the communities where they live and work. The money is managed via two funds: the Child Care Resource and Development Fund and the Elder Care Project Development Fund. The funds include $22 million for child care and $3 million for elder care, and will run from 1990 through 1994. Funding is allocated at $5 million per year.

Funding for child care began first; it was used for the development and expansion of child care centers, accreditation/licensing assistance, recruitment and training of new family child care providers, development and enhancement of programs for school-age children, as well as programs for mildly ill children. In order to receive funds, new child care centers must meet the NAEYC accreditation standards. The funds will be administered by Work/Family Directions, IBM's dependent care consultant.

In 1990, the Child Care Resource and Development Fund supported several local initiatives such as the recruitment and training of child care staff aged fifty-five and older, assistance to part-time, off-shift, and extended hours employees, a mobile infant equipment lending program, and new after-school programs. Five child care consortium centers were announced in December 1990, representing a $3.5 million investment. Then-IBM chairman John Akers said, "[This] reflects IBM's continuing response to the changing social environment affecting IBM's employees. The challenge to business is to provide employees the flexibility they need to pursue and advance their careers while minimizing the impact on their personal lives." •

AT&T Family Care Development Fund

The objectives of the AT&T Family Care Development Fund are to increase the supply and to improve the quality of child and elder care services available to AT&T employees across the country. The fund, which began in January 1990, was created by and is jointly administered by AT&T, the Communications Workers of America, and the International Brotherhood of Electrical Workers.

During its first three years, the fund granted $10 million to over 350 projects in 26 states. During 1993–1995 the fund will commit an additional $15 million.

Most of the grants available through the Family Care Development Fund are made to local community programs and initiatives in both child and elder care. Employee involvement is the foundation of the Family Care Development Fund's design. To ensure that the local projects supported by the fund respond to the needs of AT&T people, community organizations requesting grants must have an AT&T employee sponsor, or be invited to apply for funding.

Both for-profit and not-for-profit child care providers who meet quality and professional eligibility criteria can apply for grants. The fund supports a wide range of projects including expansion grants, start-up of new programs, and quality improvement grants. One initiative provides funding for any center servicing at least one AT&T employee to become NAEYC-accredited.

While community support is an important by-product of the fund's activities, grants are not made solely on the basis of community need. Funds are granted only to those projects that result in a benefit for AT&T employees. Grants are given with a preference for projects that build the supply of child care and those that serve the most employees and/or fill the greatest gap in services. •

Corporate Champions—Charlotte, North Carolina

On April 6, 1987, immediately following the annual meeting of the local child care referral agency (Child Care

156

Resources, Inc.), Bill Lee, CEO of Duke Power Company, invited representatives of Charlotte's largest employers to explore the child care issues facing the work force. He asked that the attending companies contribute to a community fund to be used to stimulate the supply of quality child care in the Charlotte-Mecklenburg area, and appoint a representative to serve on a task force to develop guidelines on dispersing the fund. Twenty companies responded, together committing over $110,000 each year for three years. The fund is maintained by the Foundation for the Carolinas, and Child Care Resources, Inc., provides staff support for the task force.

The Corporate Champions task force spent over 600 hours in meetings and individual and committee research. They determined that the fund could be used for:

1. Start-up grants for nonprofit organizations to create new programs or expand existing center-based child care programs. All new spaces created must meet the state's highest standards.

2. Start-up grants to family day care providers.

3. Training grants of $200 per caregiver to encourage existing family day care providers to participate in training.

4. Development of land deemed suitable for the creation of new child care center facilities. Identification of publically owned land suitable for the creation of new child care facilities.

5. Encouragement of local banks to work with caregivers to offer innovative financing for the expansion and creation of child care spaces ●

After the three years were over, most companies renewed their commitment to this project.

Minneapolis Success by 6®

Success by 6 is dedicated to creating a community where, by the age of six, all children's basic health and developmental needs are met, to enable them to benefit from educational and social opportunities for growth and learning.

United Way of Minneapolis Area initiated Success by 6, which is a joint effort of business, social service, government, and community leaders. In 1988, a consensus was reached on the best strategic approaches to the main barriers blocking progress toward all children under six having full opportunity for mental, physical, social, and emotional development. Two committees working in tandem for over nine months developed an action agenda. The Success by 6 Community Leaders Committee included top-level corporate leaders, government officials, union leaders, nonprofit sector leaders, and child development experts. The Success by 6 Partners Committee included representation from 33 public, private, and nonprofit institutions currently involved in serving and advocating for young children.

Success by 6 has three goals that drive the "Action Strategies":

Goal I. Build community awareness and understanding

Goal II. Improve service access

Goal III. Expand collaboration

Ten "Action Strategies" were the focus of the committees' recommendations, including:

- Promoting public awareness and understanding

- Creating a bipartisan legislative package focusing on families and young children

- Developing a strategy for employers to support workers with young children

- Coordinating neighborhood-based services for children from conception to age six, starting in one neighborhood with plans to replicate in 11 others

- Increasing the percentage of healthy births by focusing on reducing barriers to quality prenatal care

- Creating an information base to address gaps in service, including the employment and geographic variations in service resources available

Considerable progress has been made in the implementation of all the action strategies. Some of the highlights include:

- A legislative action agenda, drafted and promoted with the cooperation of 33 organizations, resulted in the passage of state legislation for an additional $55 million for children; a bill requiring cultural dynamic training for educators has passed Minnesota legislation.

- A community network designed to disseminate information and action alerts about children's legislation has been formed.

- A plan has been approved to provide the members of the Greater Minneapolis Chamber of Commerce with information on work and feedback on such issues facing member companies.

- Phillips TLC, a prenatal care and education program, was created in the Phillips neighborhood. As a result of the program, now in year three, the average infant mortality rate of participants fell to 3 percent from the neighborhood average of 21 percent.

- Eleven "Tools for Success by 6" projects have been implemented to help parents understand and encourage the healthy development of their children.

- The Hennepin County Medical Society has agreed to take a leadership role in implementing a plan to address barriers to prenatal care and successfully brought the managed care provider leadership to the table to work in partnership in addressing prenatal barriers.

- Over 60 cities around the country are developing early childhood initiatives replicating the Success by 6 Minneapolis model. ●

Kiwanis International

In 1990, Kiwanis International instituted a continuing program titled Young Children: Priority One. Each of the 8,800 clubs is asked to participate in this program by developing a project addressing a need of children, prenatal through age five. Clubs receive a Project Idea List that suggests possible projects in four areas of need:

Maternal and Infant Health. Projects include public education, development of health care services for a community, home visitation to pregnant women, and adolescent pregnancy prevention.

Child Care Development. Projects include support for a resource and referral agency, support for an early childhood development program (from a Head Start program to a family child care provider), family literacy, and public awareness.

Parent Education and Support. Projects include support of parenting classes, a helpline, child abuse prevention program, family resource library or center, home visitation program, or respite care.

Safety and Pediatric Trauma. Projects include a safety seat loan program, smoke alarm battery

checks, distribution of choke-test tubes, drown-
proofing, and education on poisons.

Kiwanis International has established an advisory
council of more than 30 organizations and individual
experts to help guide Young Children: Priority One.
Among the organizations on the council are the American
Academy of Pediatrics, American College of Obstetricians
and Gynecologists, Child Welfare League, Cooperative
Extension Service, March of Dimes, National Association
for the Education of Young Children, Reading Is
Fundamental, and YMCA.

From October 1991 to October 1992, 1,867 of 8,800
Kiwanis clubs around the world formally reported
investments totaling $4,624,441 to address the needs of
Young Children: Priority One. Examples of specific child
care projects that have been developed include: Head
Start Family Olympics, Infant/Toddler Immunization
Clinic, Boy Scouts Child Care Program, Parenting Skills
Classes, Parent Resource Center, Construction
Rehabilitation Project to provide permanent housing to
abused mothers with infants and toddlers, Preschool
Expo, Day Care Center Development, Community Task
Force for Literacy, and Saturday Storytelling. •

American Business Collaboration
for Quality Dependent Care

In September 1992, 137 companies, including 11 of the
nation's leading corporations, pledged $25.4 million to
increase the supply and improve the quality of dependent
care services for their employees. The basic principle

guiding this effort, as stated in the CEO's Statement, is "the belief that we can accomplish more by working together than by working alone."

The funds are being used to finance 300 local programs in 44 communities in 25 states and the District of Columbia, including new and expanded child care centers, programs for school-age children, in-home care for the elderly, and training for family day care providers. The 11 corporations spearheading the effort are Allstate Insurance Company, American Express, Amoco Corporation, AT&T, Eastman Kodak Company, Exxon Corporation, IBM, Johnson & Johnson, Motorola, The Travelers, and Xerox. The 44 communities involved in the collaboration range from Huntsville, Alabama, to Chicago, Illinois.

Each of the participating communities conducted a needs assessment to determine local initiatives. Examples of initiatives include: Backup Child Care Registry, Before/After School Expansion, In-Home Elder Care Companion, Recruitment and Training of Family Day Care Providers, School-Age Vacation/Holiday Project, Infant/Toddler Training Institute, and new child care centers. ●

REFERENCES

1. M. O. Steinfels, *Who's Minding the Children? The History and Politics of Day Care in America* (New York: Simon and Schuster, 1973).
2. P. K. Robins, "Federal Financing of Child Care: Alternative Approaches and Economic Implications," paper prepared for the Economic Implications and Benefits of Child Care conference, sponsored by the Child Care Action Campaign, New York, NY, January 1988.
3. P. K. Robins, 1988, p. 8.
4. P. K. Robins, 1988.

5. S. Stephan and S. Schillmoeller, *Child Care: Selected Federal Programs*, 87-303EPW, Congressional Research Service (Washington, DC: Library of Congress, 1987).

6. P. K. Robins, 1988.

7. Section 125 of the IRS Code permits employers to offer employees a choice in benefits. Section 129 of the IRS Code makes child care a nontaxable benefit, and therefore an option in flexible benefits.

8. M. Whitebook, C. Howes, and D. A. Phillips, *Who Cares? Child Care Teachers and the Quality of Care in America*, final report, National Child Care Staffing Study (Oakland, CA: Child Care Employee Project, 1990).

9. Child Care Action Campaign, *Child Care Action Campaign Special Report #1: State Employer Tax Credits for Child Care* (New York: New York University, November 1989).

10. L. W. Tentler, *Wage Earning Women: Industrial Work and Family Life in the U.S., 1900–1930* (New York: Oxford University Press, 1979), p. 161.

11. K. W. Feinstein, ed., *Working Women and Families* (Beverly Hills: Sage Publications, 1979), pp. 189–190.

12. R. M. Kanter, *Work and Family Life in the United States: A Critical Review and Agenda for Research and Policy* (New York: Russell Sage Foundation, 1977).

13. *Child Care Liability Task Force, Employer Centers and Child Care Liability Insurance* (Washington, DC: U.S. Department of Labor, December 1989), p. 14.

14. E. Galinsky, D. E. Friedman, and C. A. Hernandez, *The Corporate Reference Guide to Work-Family Programs* (New York: Families and Work Institute, 1991).

15. E. Galinsky et al., 1991.

16. E. Galinsky et al., 1991.

17. K. Christensen, *Flexible Staffing and Scheduling* (New York: The Conference Board, 1989).

18. E. Galinsky et al., 1991.

19. E. Galinsky et al., 1991.

20. E. Galinsky et al., 1991.

21. E. Galinsky et al., 1991.

22. G. Morgan, personal communication, November 1990.

23. Louis Harris and Associates, Inc., *The Philip Morris Child Care Survey* (New York: Philip Morris Companies, 1989).

CHAPTER 6

Conclusion

As U.S. companies provide child care benefits to their employees, contribute to community-based child care initiatives, and wage a campaign to reform the nation's educational system, we hope they will bear in mind the most important messages of this book:

- That child care provides a means for both education and care

- That education begins before school

- That children have the capacity to learn as soon as they are born

- That children need a warm, nurturing environment in order to reach their full potential

These realities for children underscore the importance of emphasizing quality in child care and early education as a strategy for meeting the National Education Goal of readiness for school.

WHO IS RESPONSIBLE?

While there are some who feel that only government is responsible for improving the quality of child care programs and others who assume that corporate America will pick up the slack, it is the authors' position that the solution requires partnerships among all stakeholders.

An example of such a partnership can be found in New York City, where the Temporary Commission on Early Childhood and Child Care Programs created a ten-year plan for the redesign of the delivery system for early education and care. The business leaders, government officials, and early childhood experts who served on the commission recognized the need to integrate services offered by the Agency for Child Development and the Board of Education and to focus on quality improvements.

THE CORPORATE ROLE

Corporations can play a unique role in keeping quality issues at the forefront of the child care debate and as a goal of new initiatives—whether through internal efforts or external partnerships. Figure 6.1 describes ways for companies to incorporate quality concerns into specific employer-supported child care efforts. Figure 6.2 describes ways for employers to promote quality through local, state, and national advocacy.

Our nation's child care system can also benefit from in-

Figure 6.1

WAYS TO IMPROVE QUALITY THROUGH INTERNAL COMPANY INITIATIVES

Initiative	Methods of Quality Improvement	
Parent Seminars	• Include information about selecting quality child care in employee communications such as in-house newspapers or magazines or include this information with salary checks.	• Develop seminars on how to select quality child care.
Child Care Resource and Referral	• Make certain that the service the company purchases is not merely a list of licensed programs but is a professional counseling service that helps parents identify quality indicators and regularly updates list of providers.	• Make certain that the CCR&R service includes the training of child care providers.
DCAPs	• Include information on the importance of selecting quality child care as part of the literature for the DCAP account.	• Include checklists or research data on quality along with reimbursement checks.
Vouchers	• Set guidelines for the kind of programs vouchers can be used for.	• Include regular information on quality along with voucher checks. • Increase size of voucher depending on whether program is licensed or not.
Discounts	• Provide discounts only at programs that meet quality criteria or have been accredited by NAEYC.	• Give parents using discounts regular information about quality.
On- or Near-Site Child Care	• Provide ongoing quality standards. • Offer money and assistance to help the program become accredited, or prepare for accreditation, by NAEYC.	• Develop a financing structure that allows the child care staff to be paid adequate wages. • Offer scholarships to lower-wage-earning employees so they can enroll in the quality program that is developed.
Sick or Emergency Child Care	• Ensure that all providers are trained professionals and are well enough compensated to ensure a consistency of quality care, and to eliminate turnover.	• Ensure that health and safety standards are met. In sick child care programs, care should be taken so that children are not exposed to other illnesses.
Leave	• Provide part-day and full-day time off for parents to select child care/early education programs.	• Provide part-day and full-day time off for parents to visit or participate in their children's programs and attend teacher conferences.

Source: Families and Work Institute, 1993.

Figure 6.2
WAYS TO IMPROVE QUALITY THROUGH EXTERNAL COMPANY INITIATIVES

LOCAL INITIATIVES	
Initiative	**Method of Quality Improvement**
Corporate Contributions	• Fund quality efforts in the community. • Expand corporate giving for child care beyond United Way donations. Make child care one of the priority areas in giving. In doing so, consider combining gifts for child care and early education, as Johnson & Johnson does. • Fund educational supports such as lending libraries, training programs, and conferences. • Fund efforts that help family child care providers become licensed or registered. • Subsidize salary surveys and other strategies to help raise providers' salaries. This can include providing bonuses or awards when teachers receive a CDA or other credential for years of service in the child care field, mini-grants to improve salaries and benefits, and training in budgeting.
Deployment of Corporate Expertise	• Share relevant data from company-sponsored needs assessments to assist in long-range community planning. • Share information about corporate child care programs so that other companies can model them. • Provide business expertise to help local child care programs improve quality, such as lending executives to help programs budget more efficiently, or to improve personnel policies. • Encourage employees to get involved with child care by serving on boards of directors or working to improve their own children's programs. • Use company newspapers and magazines to feature stories on involved employees and applaud their community child care contributions. • Feature stories about supportive employees in community newspapers, television and radio to serve as a role model for other companies.
Task Force	• Serve on task forces to improve the quality of local child care. • Convene local company executives, social service leaders, child care and early education experts to identify problems and pose solutions. • Replicate successful quality improvement efforts, such as Success by 6, pioneered in Minneapolis (see case study). • Participate in the National Association of Education's Full Cost of Quality Campaign, a community problem-solving effort to halt the escalating staff turnover by raising salaries.
Fund Raising	• Leverage money from other companies for joint funding efforts. Corporate Champions in Charlotte, North Carolina, is an example (see case study).
Advocacy	• Work to improve local child care standards. • Work with mayors and civic groups to remove obstacles to improving quality.

Source: Families and Work Institute, 1993.

Figure 6.2—Continued

STATE INITIATIVES	
Initiative	**Method of Quality Improvement**
Advocacy	• Urge the state to improve its standards if they fall below professionally agreed-upon criteria. • Become knowledgeable about licensing and enforcement. If regulations have no teeth (insufficient funding for staff to monitor the regulations), advocate for increased funding for the state licensing department. • Encourage the states to help programs become NAEYC-accredited.
Task Forces	• Join governors' task forces. At the end of the task forces' deliberations, help design and implement a strategic plan for measurable objectives. Reconvene in a year to make sure these objectives have been implemented and that state strategies are in place to improve the quality of child care in the state. • Form an advisory group to study the economics of the child care system in the state. The Maryland Employers Advisory Council on Child Care (see case study) is an example. • Serve as an advocate to develop new state programs to improve quality, such as salary enhancement legislation, technical and training assistance, resource and referral, grant and loan programs. • Serve as a watchdog to ensure that the state is providing sufficient money for child care, especially as welfare reform programs evolve. (Welfare reform may push nonwelfare, low-income children out of the system.) • Help eliminate barriers to keeping public schools open for before- and after-school programs.
Partnerships	• Participate in public/private partnerships to improve quality. If no public/private partnerships exist, help get them started.

FEDERAL INITIATIVES	
Initiative	**Method of Quality Improvement**
Testimony	• Testify in Congress for improved quality of child care.
Public Education	• Be a national spokesperson on the issue of quality in child care and the family-friendly workplace by appearing in the media, writing guest editorials in newspapers and magazines, and speaking at conferences.
Advocacy	• Encourage national professional, organizational and industry groups to become involved in improving the quality of child care.

Source: Families and Work Institute, 1993.

creased public awareness and understanding. Many parents and teachers already understand that education and nurturing cannot be considered separately, and the vast majority of parents and child care center directors agree that programs should promote both healthy development as well as school readiness.[1] However, much work is still needed to increase public awareness on the following:

Early education and child care should be considered together. The child care system in this country constitutes a major portion of the early childhood education system.

Improving child care means making a substantial investment in quality. The public and private sectors cannot avoid the issue of quality if they hope to improve the delivery mechanisms of child care — all of these issues are integrally related.

Education reform will not succeed unless attention is paid to children's earliest years. Successful school reform requires attention to the care and early education of infants, toddlers, and preschoolers. "Developmentally appropriate teaching" that bases early childhood education on an understanding of the way children learn, also should be applied to the way children are taught in school.

The purpose of early education and care is not simply to get children ready for school. Early education is not just readiness training, nor is preschool merely the stage before school entry. It is a time when fundamental capabilities are being developed, such as the ability to learn how to learn, to care about learning, to feel competent, to find the world an interesting place to learn about, and to turn experiences into skills and concepts into knowledge. This is also a time when social competencies are being developed: Children are learning how to work in groups, how to learn from and teach each other, how to work with adults, and how to solve social problems. It is particularly important to tackle these developmental tasks in the early years.

A PERSONAL VISION FOR THE FUTURE

Those stakeholders who have recognized the importance of child care to the education of young children and their readiness for school have come to realize that improving child care quality cannot be achieved without significant changes in the way child care is delivered at the community level.

There are a number of models for creating a more coherent delivery system for quality child care and early education that are either in use or being tested. Examples include the resource center model,[2] the School of the 21st Century,[3] and the French model.[4]

The authors' own research has led us, in conjunction with Joan Lombardi, an early childhood policy analyst, to develop a personal vision for an early childhood* delivery system based on the concept of public-private partnerships, called the Quality Early Childhood Model. This model is predicated on the notion that no one sector — business, government, parents, or professionals in the child care field —

*Because we see education and care as inextricably linked, we use the term *early childhood* to refer to both.

171

can, by themselves, make the kind of changes necessary to develop a quality delivery system at the community level. Partnerships are needed among all of the key stakeholders.

KEY FEATURES OF THE QUALITY
EARLY CHILDHOOD MODEL

The authors envision a community-based child care system that has three key components:

- A network of programs that emphasize both care and education

- Community-based child and family resource centers

- A community-wide leadership group

This model does not require the development of a whole new set of programs. Instead, it envisions weaving together those that already exist and strengthening and expanding them where needed.

A NETWORK OF PROGRAMS

The authors' model would maintain the diversity of the current system by offering families real choices among a variety of good-quality programs (including full-day and half-day child development programs in centers, in family child care homes, in Head Start programs, and in schools) that could best meet the needs of both children and parents.

This model would resemble elementary and secondary

172

schooling less than it does higher education. Like the colleges and universities of this country, this early childhood system would be based on standards, accountability, and public and private support. We envision a system in which fees are more like tuition, rather than the sliding fee scales often used currently to accommodate the range of parent incomes. These "tuition fees" would represent the full cost of quality care. If parents could not afford this cost, assistance could be provided (as in the state of Hawaii) through public and private scholarships. Unlike the higher education system, local programs would form linkages to one another. Family child care homes could exist as satellites of schools or child care centers. Staff of various kinds of programs could meet together and share resources. Programs could be linked both to social and health services and to the public schools. This model also would encourage family-centered programming by building partnerships between parents and professionals and increasing parental involvement.

CHILD AND FAMILY RESOURCE CENTERS

The hub of the Quality Early Childhood Model would be resource centers in the community to provide a wide range of support services to families, early childhood professionals, and employers. These resources could grow out of an existing program such as a Head Start center, family support program, library, or community agency. Such resource centers could provide parent support and education, one-stop access for locating and selecting early childhood programs, assistance with scholarships, and access to other needed services. They could also provide support for the local early childhood community such as bulk purchasing or training, which could be accomplished with linkages to the higher education system. Finally, these resource centers could provide assistance to employers involved in child care and early education.

COMMUNITY LEADERSHIP

In the authors' vision, the effectiveness of the Quality Early Childhood Model would depend on having an active and committed group of community leaders to guide the system. The Leadership Group would be drawn from a wide range of stakeholders, including early childhood professionals, business, labor, schools, religious and philanthropic groups, local government, and allied social services. Among its functions, the Leadership Group could conduct a child care needs assessment, or audit, for the community, addressing such issues as quality, adequacy of supply, and funding as well as develop goals, help raise money, and design a system for accountability.

COMMUNITY AND STATE EXAMPLES

Elements of the Quality Early Childhood Model envisioned by the authors are being adapted and implemented in various communities and states around the country. In a number of areas, planning groups are working to create a comprehensive system, establish resource centers and community-wide training, establish scholarship programs, and create leadership groups. Initiatives in Indiana, Colorado, Texas, Hawaii, and New York City illustrate some of the approaches being used (see boxes).

COMMUNITY-WIDE PLANNING TO CREATE A COMPREHENSIVE SYSTEM: INDIANA

In January of 1991, Governor Evan Bayh presented the Step Ahead initiative in his State of the State address. This initiative was passed by the Indiana general assembly with bipartisan support. Step Ahead was introduced to address the recognized need in Indiana for a collaborative approach to ensure a seamless service delivery system to families and children. The goal of this effort is that by the year 2000 all children in Indiana will have access to the developmental health and education programs that will ensure they enter school ready to learn. The main focus of the Step Ahead initiative is to support efforts of Indiana's local counties to reduce duplication and fragmentation of services. Step Ahead is part of what is now the Division of Family and Children, Bureau of Child Development.

At the state level, Step Ahead is a system for coordinating funding streams to facilitate access to comprehensive services at the local level. The state's role is to remove barriers to local communities, providers, and families so that matching these groups to funding sources becomes an administrative issue rather than a problem for the provider of the affected family. Step Ahead's key principles state that services must be: family centered, mutually beneficial to all who invest, diverse, focused on parents as a child's first and most important teacher, engaged person to person, and provided within a seamless continuum of care.

Indiana's 92 counties quickly responded to the Step

continued

Ahead process. Currently all are in the Step Ahead planning stage, which involves convening all appropriate representatives at the county level to form the local Step Ahead Council. Councils include but are not limited to: health services, education, child care and early childhood development programs, Head Start, educational and employment services for adults, community service organizations, religious organizations, social welfare organizations, and business and industry sectors. Each county's plan will address such things as the upgrade of quality; available, accessible, and affordable services for families; coordination and enhancement of existing services; and the leverage of funds and resources. •

COMMUNITY-WIDE PLANNING TO CREATE A COMPREHENSIVE EARLY CHILDHOOD SYSTEM, RESOURCE CENTERS, AND SYSTEM-WIDE TRAINING: COLORADO

Also using community-wide planning as a tool, the state of Colorado is developing resource centers and an early childhood training system. Their initiative is called the Strategic Plan for Colorado Families and Children. Its purpose is to create a service delivery system based on building family strengths rather than remediating family crises. This plan was formulated when state policy makers and First Lady Bea Romer attended an academy

continued

convened by the Council of Governors' Policy Advisors. It was then revised based on community information obtained through seven regional citizens' forums throughout the state.

At the state level, several groups have been set up to make this vision a reality: (1) The Commission on Families and Children, a 30-member group to advise the governor; and (2) the Families and Children's Cabinet Council, made up of heads of agencies serving children and families to promote interagency problem solving and policy development.

When an analysis of the budget revealed that the largest proportion of state spending was on remediation and that there was enormous duplication of service, monies were reallocated to enact the vision. Greater system accountability was also built in.

The vision calls for the development of Family Centers to provide one-stop access to service for families, including family support, health, child care, resource and referral, etc. The state issued a Request for Proposal (RFP) to create these centers, requiring that they be located in high-risk communities but serve all community members regardless of income. Application for funding could not be by a single agency, but the community at large, including the superintendent of schools or a principal of a neighborhood school, the county social services director, the county health department director, an elected official, a business representative, a service provider, and at least two parents who might use the services of a

continued

177

family center. In 1992, eight communities received planning grants of $30,000 for the six-month start-up phase.

In addition, Governor Roy Romer has established an Early Childhood Professional Standards Task Force, which, in August 1992, presented a set of recommendations to construct a career development model. This model ensures that "everyone working with young children has the same core knowledge and competencies regardless of where they work." Thus, there will be standardization of professional requirements, bridging noncredit and credited programs, and the creation of incentives that address wages, benefits, and status issues. •

VOUCHERS: HAWAII

In 1989, the Hawaii State Legislature created the Preschool Open Doors Project. It provides tuition and fee subsidies for children ages three and a half to five to attend preschool programs of their choice. This project assists low- and moderate-income families in designated geographic areas with the amount of assistance varying by family income up to a maximum of $350 a month. •

SEAMLESS FUNDING, ONE-STOP SHOPPING: TEXAS

In Texas, Child Care Management Services (CCMS) has been developed to merge and manage multiple funding sources in order to improve the quality and quantity of child care.

This initiative began after a meeting held by Texas Department of Human Services in 1989 to create a vision of a comprehensive system of information and fiscal management. This led the state to rearrange its child care regions and develop a one-year phase-in period.

The system works as follows: CCMS competitively obtains contracts with agencies in the 27 regions. These subcontracting agencies then form vendor relations with licensed centers and registered family child care homes. A parent needing care contacts the agency, which provides information about programs and funding assistance (through pooled resources) and then actually secures the care. In addition, CCMS agencies recruit, train, and pay providers. All agencies use a single, comprehensive computer system.

Since its beginning, the child care and development budget has increased from $37 million in 1989 to $178 million in 1992. These include local, state, and federal revenues. •

LEADERSHIP GROUPS

The New York City Early Education Leadership Group was created to implement the vision created by the Temporary Commission on Early Education and Child Care Programs in their final recommendations to Mayor David Dinkins in February 1992. Comprised of CEOs and public sector leaders, the Leadership Group is facilitating the involvement of the business community in improving early education and child care. Plans and specific projects are being developed to support, measure, and publicize progress each year toward the ten-year program improvement goals developed by the Temporary Commission. Private-sector funds will be raised to demonstrate solutions, encourage innovation, and evaluate models, and to promote a positive image for early childhood services. •

THE NEED FOR FURTHER WORK

Since 1990, two national studies have been published that confirm the need for policy debates in child care to focus on quality.[5, 6] These studies conclude that quality has been sacrificed in programs serving the nation's youngest children in order to create more slots at a price that parents can pay—the great trade-off in child care.

We already know a good deal about quality, what it is, how to identify it, and to a growing extent, how it affects children's development. By ignoring the fact that children are learning long before they enter school, those who are attempting to reform the public school system are missing important opportunities and, perhaps, even jeopardizing education reform itself.

Despite our understanding of quality early childhood care, we do not know how to make quality affordable or how to equitably balance affordability and quality. Until we know more about these issues, we will not be able to resolve the trade-off between high quality on the one hand and affordability and supply on the other; nor will we be able to resolve how best to balance the differing child care needs of parents, employers, society, and most important, children.

Much of this problem results from having very little conclusive research on the costs and benefits of quality to individuals or society. Further study in this area, particularly by economists, is much needed and would be much welcomed in the child care field.

In the policy arena, there is a very simple first step to improve child care that has not been fully taken: to recognize child care as an integral part of our nation's early education system and to develop new strategies for improving its quality.

REFERENCES

1. B. Willer, S. Hofferth, E. E. Kisker, P. Divine-Hawkins, E. Farquhar, and F. B. Glanz, *The Demand and Supply of Child Care in 1990* (Washington, DC: National Association for the Education of Young Children: U.S. Department of Health and Human Services, Administration for Children, Youth, and Families; U.S. Department of Education, Office of the Undersecretary, 1991).

2. G. Morgan, *Two Visions: The Future of Day Care and Early Childhood Programs*, unpublished manuscript, 1987.

3. E. F. Zigler and M. Lang, "The School of the 21st Century: A Step Toward a Unified System of Child Care and Family Support," in *Child Care Choices* (New York: The Free Press, 1991), pp. 190–214.

4. G. Richardson and E. Marx, *A Welcome for Every Child, How France Achieves Quality Child Care: Practical Ideas for the United States* (New York: The French-American Foundation, 1989).

5. S. L. Hofferth, A. Brayfield, S. Deitch, and P. Holcomb, *The National Child Care Survey, 1990* (Washington, DC: The Urban Institute, 1991).

6. E. E. Kisker, S. L. Hofferth, D. A. Phillips, and E. Farquhar, *A Profile of Child Care Settings: Early Education and Care in 1990*, Vol. 1. (Princeton: Mathematica Policy Research, Inc., 1991).

SUGGESTIONS FOR FURTHER READING

For additional examples and ideas on innovation in care and education, see:

1. Blank, M. and Lombardi, J. *Forging New Relationships Through Collaboration: Towards Improved Services for Children and Families*, a policy brief based on the Eighth Annual Symposium of the A. L. Mailman Family Foundation. Washington, DC: Institute for Educational Leadership, 1991.

2. Friedman, D. E. and King, M. *Public-Private Partnerships for Child Care*. New York: Families and Work Institute, 1991.

3. Kagan, S. L. *United We Stand*. New York: Teachers College Press, 1991.

4. National Association of State Boards of Education, *Caring Communities: Supporting Young Children and Families*. Alexandria, VA: National Association of State Boards of Education, 1991.

5. National Governors' Association, *Every Child Ready for School: A Report of the Action Team on School Readiness*. Washington, DC: NGA, 1992.

6. Sachar, S. J., Heller, A., Hill, M. H., Sullivan, P. F., *From Homes to Classrooms to Workrooms*. Washington, DC: National Governors' Association, 1992.

7. Sugarman, J. M. *Building Early Childhood Systems: A Resource Handbook*. Washington, DC: Child Welfare League of America, 1991.

Index

Page numbers of charts, graphs, and boxes appear in italics.

187

Resources for Child Caring, St.
Paul, MN, 98
Romer, Bea, 176
Romer, Roy, 178

Scarr, S., 24
Schillmoeller, S., 116
School age children, child care
for, 40
School failure, 1, 8
School of the Twenty-First
Century model, 171
School performance improvement
and quality child care, 73
Schwartz, Felice, 17–18
Sick children
care for, 39, 62–63
employer provided care,
133–34, 148–49
"get well" rooms for, 68
Skadden Arps, 150
Social development of child, 24,
25, 26, 27–28, 78
Social Service Block Grant, *115*,
116, 117
Social services, need for
coordination with early
education services, 3, 7, 173
Social skills, teaching of, 26
Society, benefits to of high-quality
child care, 58–59, 72–79, *78,
79*, 108–10
Special education, relationship to
child care, 59, 73, 79
Staff
and behavior management
techniques, 26
career ladder for, 96
center directors, 96
-child ratio, 27–28, *29*, 51, 52,
54, *54*, 55, 106–8, *108*
interactions with children,
27–28, 45
and parent relationship, 30–31
shortage of, 45
training/education of, 28, 30,
52, 96, 145

turnover, 6, 27, 39, 45–46,
48–49, *49, 50*, 87, 106
types of, *20*
wages, 6, 39, 46–47, *49*, 87, 96,
97
Stephan, S., 116
Stress
of children in low-quality care,
25
of employees and child care
problems, 8, 58, 61, 66
and job performance, 66
-related health problems and
difficulty in obtaining child
care, 65
Subsidization
for child care, 89, 144–45
1990 Federal Child Care
Initiatives, *119–20*
reasons for, 108–10
of salaries, 105–6, *168*
state programs in operation,
175–80
Syracuse Family Development
Research Program, 30–31, 76

Target Stores, 103, 133, 145–46
Tax credits for child care, *115,*
116, 117, *120*, 121, 136
Tax Exclusion for Employer-
Provided Care, *115*
Teacher(s)
in accredited programs, 25
in child care settings, 6
-child ratio, 27–28, *29*, 31, 51,
52, 54, *54*, 55
-child relationship, 23–27, 45
interactions with children,
27–28
master teachers, use of, 96, *97*
and parent relationship, 30–31
in public school programs, 6
sensitivity of, 28
shortages of, 46
social skills teaching, 26
training/education of, 28, 30,
46, 52